DISCARD

D1651324

Black A M

A M

DETROIT PUBLIC LIBRARY

CL

DATE DUE

MAY 13 1993

MAY 10 1994

MAR 23 1996

FEB 24 1998

MAR 03 2001

WALTER WHITE

BLACK AMERICANS OF ACHIEVEMENT

WALTER WHITE

Jane Fraser

Senior Consulting Editor
Nathan Irvin Huggins
Director
W.E.B. Du Bois Institute for Afro-American Research
Harvard University

CHELSEA HOUSE PUBLISHERS
New York   Philadelphia

Chelsea House Publishers
Editor-in-Chief Remmel Nunn
Managing Editor Karyn Gullen Browne
Copy Chief Juliann Barbato
Picture Editor Adrian G. Allen
Art Director Maria Epes
Deputy Copy Chief Mark Rifkin
Assistant Art Director Noreen Romano
Manufacturing Manager Gerald Levine
Systems Manager Lindsey Ottman
Production Manager Joseph Romano
Production Coordinator Marie Claire Cebrián

Black Americans of Achievement
Senior Editor Richard Rennert

Staff for WALTER WHITE
Text Editor Marian W. Taylor
Copy Editor Brian Sookram
Editorial Assistant Michele Haddad
Picture Reseacher Patricia Burns
Designer Ghila Krajzman
Cover Illustration Patti Oleon

Copyright © 1991 by Chelsea House Publishers, a division of Main Line Book Co. All rights reserved. Printed and bound in the United States of America.

First Printing

1 3 5 7 9 8 6 4 2

Library of Congress Cataloging-in-Publication Data
Fraser, Jane
    Walter White—civil rights leader/ by Jane Fraser.
      p. cm.—(Black Americans of achievement)
    Includes bibliographical references.
    Summary: Discusses the life and achievements of the civil rights leader who served as secretary of the NAACP from 1931 until his death.
    ISBN 1-55546-617-6
      0-7910-0253-5 (pbk.)
    1. White, Walter Francis, 1893–1955—Juvenile literature. 2. Afro-Americans—Biography—Juvenile literature. 3. Civil rights workers—United States—Biography—Juvenile literature. 4. National Association for the Advancement of Colored People—Biography—Juvenile literature. 5. Afro-Americans—Civil rights—Juvenile literature. 6. Civil rights movements—United States—History—20th century—Juvenile literature. [1. White, Walter Francis, 1893–1955. 2. Civil rights workers. 3. National Association for the Advancement of Colored People. 4. Afro-Americans—Biography.]
I. Title. II. Series.
E185.97.W6F73 1990
323'.092—dc20   90-1768
[B]   CIP
[92]   AC

Frontispiece: *Walter White (right, facing audience) addresses an interracial rally at the Lincoln Memorial in Washington, D.C., during World War II.*

CONTENTS

On Achievement 7
Coretta Scott King

1
A Stranger in Town 11

2
"I Knew Who I Was" 19

3
*"Decide What's Right
and Don't Falter"* 29

4
Lives on the Line 37

5
"Among the Hunted" 49

6
"Difficult Days" 57

7
Capital Gains 71

8
Battlefronts 81

9
"I've Got Work to Do" 93

Chronology 107

Further Reading 108

Index 109

BLACK AMERICANS OF ACHIEVEMENT

RALPH ABERNATHY
civil rights leader

MUHAMMAD ALI
heavyweight champion

RICHARD ALLEN
religious leader and social activist

LOUIS ARMSTRONG
musician

ARTHUR ASHE
tennis great

JOSEPHINE BAKER
entertainer

JAMES BALDWIN
author

BENJAMIN BANNEKER
scientist and mathematician

AMIRI BARAKA
poet and playwright

COUNT BASIE
bandleader and composer

ROMARE BEARDEN
artist

JAMES BECKWOURTH
frontiersman

MARY MCLEOD BETHUNE
educator

BLANCHE BRUCE
politician

RALPH BUNCHE
diplomat

GEORGE WASHINGTON CARVER
botanist

CHARLES CHESNUTT
author

BILL COSBY
entertainer

PAUL CUFFE
merchant and abolitionist

FATHER DIVINE
religious leader

FREDERICK DOUGLASS
abolitionist editor

CHARLES DREW
physician

W.E.B. DU BOIS
scholar and activist

PAUL LAURENCE DUNBAR
poet

KATHERINE DUNHAM
dancer and choreographer

MARIAN WRIGHT EDELMAN
civil rights leader and lawyer

DUKE ELLINGTON
bandleader and composer

RALPH ELLISON
author

JULIUS ERVING
basketball great

JAMES FARMER
civil rights leader

ELLA FITZGERALD
singer

MARCUS GARVEY
black-nationalist leader

DIZZY GILLESPIE
musician

PRINCE HALL
social reformer

W. C. HANDY
father of the blues

WILLIAM HASTIE
educator and politician

MATTHEW HENSON
explorer

CHESTER HIMES
author

BILLIE HOLIDAY
singer

JOHN HOPE
educator

LENA HORNE
entertainer

LANGSTON HUGHES
poet

ZORA NEALE HURSTON
author

JESSE JACKSON
civil rights leader and politician

JACK JOHNSON
heavyweight champion

JAMES WELDON JOHNSON
author

SCOTT JOPLIN
composer

BARBARA JORDAN
politician

MARTIN LUTHER KING, JR.
civil rights leader

ALAIN LOCKE
scholar and educator

JOE LOUIS
heavyweight champion

RONALD MCNAIR
astronaut

MALCOLM X
militant black leader

THURGOOD MARSHALL
Supreme Court justice

ELIJAH MUHAMMAD
religious leader

JESSE OWENS
champion athlete

CHARLIE PARKER
musician

GORDON PARKS
photographer

SIDNEY POITIER
actor

ADAM CLAYTON POWELL, JR.
political leader

LEONTYNE PRICE
opera singer

A. PHILIP RANDOLPH
labor leader

PAUL ROBESON
singer and actor

JACKIE ROBINSON
baseball great

BILL RUSSELL
basketball great

JOHN RUSSWURM
publisher

SOJOURNER TRUTH
antislavery activist

HARRIET TUBMAN
antislavery activist

NAT TURNER
slave revolt leader

DENMARK VESEY
slave revolt leader

MADAME C. J. WALKER
entrepreneur

BOOKER T. WASHINGTON
educator

HAROLD WASHINGTON
politician

WALTER WHITE
civil rights leader and author

RICHARD WRIGHT
author

ON ACHIEVEMENT

Coretta Scott King

BEFORE YOU BEGIN this book, I hope you will ask yourself what the word excellence means to you. I think that it's a question we should all ask, and keep asking as we grow older and change. Because the truest answer to it should never change. When you think of excellence, perhaps you think of success at work; or of becoming wealthy; or meeting the right person, getting married, and having a good family life.

Those important goals are worth striving for, but there is a better way to look at excellence. As Martin Luther King, Jr., said in one of his last sermons, "I want you to be first in love. I want you to be first in moral excellence. I want you to be first in generosity. If you want to be important, wonderful. If you want to be great, wonderful. But recognize that he who is greatest among you shall be your servant."

My husband, Martin Luther King, Jr., knew that the true meaning of achievement is service. When I met him, in 1952, he was already ordained as a Baptist preacher and was working towards a doctoral degree at Boston University. I was studying at the New England Conservatory and dreamed of accomplishments in music. We married a year later, and after I graduated the following year we moved to Montgomery, Alabama. We didn't know it then, but our notions of achievement were about to undergo a dramatic change.

You may have read or heard about what happened next. What began with the boycott of a local bus line grew into a national movement, and by the time he was assassinated in 1968 my husband had fashioned a black movement powerful enough to shatter forever the practice of racial segregation. What you may not have read about is where he got his method for resisting injustice without compromising his religious beliefs.

He adopted the strategy of nonviolence from a man of a different race, who lived in a distant country, and even practiced a different religion. The man was Mahatma Gandhi, the great leader of India, who devoted his life to serving humanity in the spirit of love and nonviolence. It was in these principles that Martin discovered his method for social reform. More than anything else, those two principles were the key to his achievements.

This book is about black Americans who served society through the excellence of their achievements. It forms a part of the rich history of black men and women in America—a history of stunning accomplishments in every field of human endeavor, from literature and art to science, industry, education, diplomacy, athletics, jurisprudence, even polar exploration.

Not all of the people in this history had the same ideals, but I think you will find something that all of them have in common. Like Martin Luther King, Jr., they all decided to become "drum majors" and serve humanity. In that principle—whether it was expressed in books, inventions, or song—they found something outside themselves to use as a goal and a guide. Something that showed them a way to serve others, instead of living only for themselves.

Reading the stories of these courageous men and women not only helps us discover the principles that we will use to guide our own lives but also teaches us about our black heritage and about America itself. It is crucial for us to know the heroes and heroines of our history and to realize that the price we paid in our struggle for equality in America was dear. But we must also understand that we have gotten as far as we have partly because America's democratic system and ideals made it possible.

We are still struggling with racism and prejudice. But the great men and women in this series are a tribute to the spirit of our democratic ideals and the system in which they have flourished. And that makes their stories special and worth knowing.

WALTER WHITE

1

A STRANGER IN TOWN

THE LYNCHING WAS a week old when, on a chilly February day in 1918, the stranger appeared in Estill Springs, Tennessee. He was a small, fair-haired man with blue eyes—clearly a fellow southerner but, to the townsmen gathered around the coal stove in the country store, an outsider nonetheless.

When the newcomer approached the circle of men in the store, he began to explain that he had come to town with the idea of buying a piece of land nearby and had taken a room at the local boardinghouse. His casual manner soon put the Tennesseans at ease.

Satisfied that they had a sympathetic audience, the Estill Springs men offered the stranger a seat and began to brag about the recent lynching. It seemed that they had really taught a lesson to that Jim McIlherron. A black sharecropper, McIlherron had received a brutal beating for questioning his employer about the amount of his pay. This use of violence was not uncommon in itself: In the South of 1918, blacks

Robed and hooded Ku Klux Klan members assemble for a 1924 meeting in Beckley, West Virginia. Founded in Tennessee in 1866, the self-styled "invisible empire" aimed at asserting post–Civil War white supremacy by terrorizing, beating, and even murdering black Americans.

were so economically dependent on whites that they took physical abuse as a fact of life. What was uncommon was McIlherron's reaction to the beating: He had struck back in self-defense.

After that, the townsmen told the stranger, rounding up a crowd had taken no time at all. They had chained the sharecropper to a stake, surrounded it with a good pile of kerosene-soaked wood, and lighted a match. Then they stood back to enjoy the show. McIlherron, they said with satisfaction, had burned slowly.

The men laughed when they talked about the farmer for whom they had performed this service; he was known as a dishonest bully, and no one liked him much. Still, it was every man's duty to help his neighbor. "Any time a nigger hits a white man," remarked one of the men to the stranger, "he's gotta be handled or else all the niggers will get out of hand." They had burned Jim McIlherron in the name of brotherhood.

Many years later, the visitor recalled that he had listened to the story of the lynching very carefully. Laughing when the men laughed, looking righteously angry when they did, he put on a convincing show. He knew if he showed his true feelings or, worse, revealed his true identity, he might meet the same fate as Jim McIlherron.

The stranger who sat by the stove that day in Estill Springs was Walter White, assistant secretary of the National Association for the Advancement of Colored People (NAACP). Despite his blond hair and blue eyes—and his name—Walter White was black. He had come to Estill Springs specifically to investigate the McIlherron murder.

In that year, White's first with the NAACP, southern blacks needed advocates badly. The year before, white lynch mobs had shot, hanged, or burned to death 48 blacks; the following year, the

Walter Francis White was a 24-year-old assistant secretary to the National Association for the Advancement of Colored People (NAACP) when he investigated a 1918 lynching in Estill Springs, Tennessee. Outwardly calm at the time, White later admitted he was terrified: If the Tennessee lynchers had recognized him as a black man, he might have met the same fate as did their recent victim.

toll would rise to 63. Although racial violence occurred throughout the United States at that time, most of it took place in the South, the region that had practiced black slavery until the end of the Civil War in 1865.

In the Reconstruction period that followed the war, federal troops—some of them black—imposed an uneasy peace on the South. Always haunted by the fear of a black revolt, white southerners writhed at the sight of black men in blue uniforms. They were even more appalled by the prospect of dealing with

Clearly satisfied with its night's work, a mob surrounds the charred body of William Brown, a young black man burned to death in Omaha, Nebraska, in 1919. Like the murder of Jim McIlherron, which White had investigated in Tennessee a year earlier, Brown's lynching went unpunished.

blacks as equals, but under northern military occupation, they had little choice. Protected by the Union soldiers, blacks voted in local and national elections, and many ran successfully for political office. In 1877, however, the government withdrew its troops, and the tide began to turn.

Determined to regain control of their world, whites set about sweeping away all traces of Reconstruction and its moves toward racial equality. To keep blacks "in their place"—away from polling booths, out of public schools, and in a position of economic inferiority—they relied on threats, violence, and soon, the segregation laws that came to be labeled Jim Crow.

By the 1880s, white-robed Ku Klux Klan members roamed the countryside, hunting down and punishing blacks who tried to claim their rights as citizens. Floggings, lynchings, and unexplained disappearances became regular occurrences in black communities. And across the South, local officials made voting so difficult—and so dangerous—for blacks that most gave up trying.

In one former Confederate state after another, legislatures passed laws requiring separation of the races in all areas of life. These Jim Crow statutes went to bizarre extremes: Atlanta courts even kept a separate Bible for the swearing in of black witnesses. In 1896, the United States Supreme Court upheld the nation's Jim Crow laws in the celebrated case of *Plessy v. Ferguson*.

Plessy began when Homer Plessy, a black man, refused to move to a segregated railroad car in Louisiana. Convicted by a Louisiana judge (Ferguson) of breaking a state law calling for segregated public transportation, Plessy appealed. The Louisiana statute, he claimed, violated the Constitution's Fourteenth Amendment, which guarantees "equal protection under the law." The Court ruled against Plessy, asserting that as long as the separate facilities for blacks were "equal" to those for whites, the Fourteenth Amendment guarantee was satisfied.

The Supreme Court's approval of this "separate but equal" doctrine set a precedent (a legal decision that serves as a pattern in future cases) and opened the door to even more Jim Crow laws. From this point on, segregation was the law of the land—particularly, of course, in the South.

But the post–Civil War South feared more than integration; it also saw newly free blacks as an economic threat. Most southerners, white and black, eked out a living as farmhands and sharecroppers. To poor whites, the new black work force offered frightening competition for already meager jobs. Many southern politicians capitalized on these fears, using "white supremacy" as a rallying cry and intensifying the already explosive racial situation.

As southern antiblack attitudes hardened, lynching became an acceptable means of achieving swift "justice" for whites. Sensationalist southern newspapers, which provided a steady diet of reports about real or imagined black crimes, helped accelerate the violence. The most often replayed—and the most inflammatory—theme was the alleged rape of white women by blacks. The very idea of such a crime struck at the heart of many southern "gentlemen," allowing them to justify violence as chivalry. Investigations rarely followed lynchings of blacks who had been accused of rape, and the few lynchers who were brought to trial could count on speedy "not guilty" verdicts from all-white juries. Lynching thus earned a kind of unwritten legal approval.

These violent acts were sometimes even treated as public spectacles, attended by ordinarily "respectable" people. This chilling account was reported at an NAACP board meeting in 1911:

> WHEREAS, the Press Dispatches show that one M. Potter, a colored man, charged with killing a white man, was taken from the jail at Livermore, Ky., last week, and taken to the town Opera House, and tied on the stage, and that an admission fee was charged to witness the lynching, the prices ranging from those usually charged for orchestra and gallery seats, and that a feature of the lynching was that the audience was allowed to shoot at the suspended body of the victim, and, as in the words of the Press reports, "Those who bought orchestra seats had the privilege of emptying their six shooters at the swaying form above them, but the gallery occupants were limited to one shot."

This was the world in which Jim McIlherron had dared to stand up and defend himself, the world that had taken fast, frightful vengeance for that act. And this was the world that Walter White faced when he calmly walked into the Estill Springs general store on that February day in 1918.

Recalling the experience in his 1948 autobiography, *A Man Called White*, he admitted being terrified as his train approached Estill Springs. "I knew I would be given short shrift if McIlherron's murderers found out why I was there," he said, "[but] I believed I would have been subjected to even greater fury for the sin of 'passing' for a white man."

No one was ever prosecuted for McIlherron's killing. But White's report, he noted, "created a modest sensation, particularly when my Estill Springs informants discovered that not only was I not a prospective buyer of land but a Negro who had been housed and fed in their local hotel." Best of all, White's account created a wave of horror about lynching and, hoped its author, added to the small "number of Americans who dared to speak out against the crime."

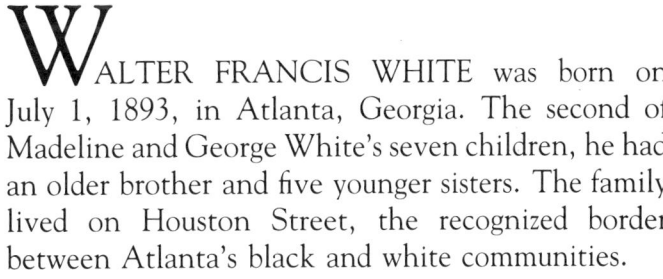

2

"I KNEW WHO I WAS"

WALTER FRANCIS WHITE was born on July 1, 1893, in Atlanta, Georgia. The second of Madeline and George White's seven children, he had an older brother and five younger sisters. The family lived on Houston Street, the recognized border between Atlanta's black and white communities.

Although the area had deteriorated over the years, the Whites' eight-room, two-story house stood as testimony to their industry: George White, a mail carrier, regularly repainted it and kept the lawn neatly trimmed and the picket fence whitewashed. Inside, former schoolteacher Madeline White, a stickler for cleanliness, washed, dusted, and polished every object within her reach, from dining room table to untidy child.

It was not easy to raise a family on a postman's small salary, but the Whites were resourceful people. George White supplemented his wages by renting out a little house he had built on their property, and Madeline White managed the household budget with care and skill. None of the children, Walter White said later, ever noticed a lack of money.

Second-grader Walter White (second row from top, standing next to teacher Lizzie M. Coleman) joins his classmates at the Houston Street School, Atlanta's first black public school, in 1900. During White's boyhood, the city offered black children no education beyond the eighth grade.

In the close-knit White family, material possessions were less valued than things of the spirit: friends, family, and faith. For the White household, Sunday was the Lord's day, a quiet time of contemplation and rest. House rules called for reading the Bible and behaving quietly, which put a major crimp in Walter's normal life-style. For a young and energetic boy, Sunday was a day to be endured, not enjoyed.

Each Sabbath began in the living room, where one of the children read a chapter from the Bible. Then, while everyone knelt on the wooden floor, George White gave God a lengthy update on the family's weekly activities. Walter found this part of the service hard on his bony knees, but fidgeting was strictly forbidden; no matter how stealthily he shifted to a sitting position, his father always noticed. George White's stern gaze did wonders for his son's powers of endurance.

Consumed with curiosity about the world around him, Walter asked questions constantly. As soon as he learned to read, he started in on his family's small collection of books, then moved on to the church library. There, he devoured all of Shakespeare's plays and most of the works of 19th-century novelists Charles Dickens, William Thackeray, and Anthony Trollope. Walter's intensive reading was encouraged both by his former-schoolteacher mother and his father, whose dream of a college education had met defeat many years earlier.

Like his son, George White had shown an early passion for learning. When he finished the eighth grade—the last one provided to black children by the state of Georgia—he went on to Atlanta University, which offered high school instruction for gifted black teenagers. With loans from his parents and income from many odd jobs, George finished four years of high school, then entered the university. During his freshman year, however, both his parents died, leaving him with heavy debts and forcing him to leave college.

Obliged to find a steady job, George White decided to apply for the position of mail carrier, at that time one of the safest and best-paid positions available to southern black men. He took the postal examination, passed with flying colors, and made up his mind to succeed at his new trade. In 43 years as a mail carrier, he would never miss a day of work and would be late only once, on a day when a freak blizzard paralyzed the rest of Atlanta.

George White gave up his dream of finishing college, but he vowed to give his children the education he had missed. Practicing self-sacrifice and sharp economies, he and his wife managed to send all seven of their children through college. But he started Walter's education long before his university years.

Every day after school, Walter joined his father on his mail route. Perched on the buggy seat, the two engaged in a long-running series of formal debates, which demanded careful strategy and informed argument. Whenever Walter seemed hazy about his subject, his father sent him to the church library. These daily intellectual games taught the boy how to think clearly and how to form a valid argument, lessons that would aid him throughout his life.

They were probably also the most valuable part of Walter's schooling. Rather than improving since his father's day, the quality of education for black children in Georgia had declined. Walter attended one of Atlanta's dilapidated black schools, presided over by well-meaning but badly undertrained teachers. He worked hard, however, and like his father, went on to high school and college.

Madeline White, blond and blue eyed, passed her looks along to her son Walter. She also passed on to

White went to work at Atlanta's stately Piedmont Hotel in 1905. The hotel manager liked the energetic 12-year-old bellboy but withdrew his offer of a promotion when he discovered the young man's race. "My guests would leave," he told White, "if they found out that you were colored."

him her deep pride in her black heritage. Although all the family members were so light complexioned that they could easily have passed for white, they never even considered it. Many light-skinned blacks escaped the burdens of racial bigotry by "passing," but George and Madeline White had no desire to lose themselves—or their children—in the white world.

The Whites' pale skin did present them with problems, however: Just as their home stood midway between the white and black districts of Atlanta, their skin color placed them midway between the two races. Like the rest of the South, Atlanta required blacks to sit in the back of the streetcars. But when Walter and his family sat in the black section, they received incredulous stares and insulting remarks from the whites at the front of the cars. On the other hand, if they sat in the white section, black neighbors criticized them for trying to pass. After years of struggling with this problem, George White made one of his few extravagant purchases—and one of his few concessions to bigotry: He bought a horse and buggy to transport his family in peace. The equipment brought no great joy to Walter, who was given the job of keeping it clean and greased, but his father loved it. One day, Walter remembered, he caught him gently stroking the side of the carriage. "It was the one moment of his life," said Walter, "when I saw him extract joy from anything except complete selfless service to his family and his God." Noticing his son, George White withdrew his hand abruptly. "The surrey is awfully dusty," he said gruffly. "Get a cloth and wipe it off."

In 1905, 12-year-old Walter landed a thrilling job: bellboy at Atlanta's elegant Piedmont Hotel. The salary—one dollar per day plus tips—seemed too good to be true. Just as exciting was his splendid purple uniform, heavily weighted with brass buttons and gold braid. Walter enjoyed bounding around the hotel, guiding guests to their rooms and bellowing out messages in the lobby.

Working in the hotel also gave Walter a surprising and disturbing view of white people's life-styles. "In the new job," he recalled in his autobiography, "I began with startling speed my education in the facts of life and . . . in the ways of white folks. What I saw and heard [at the hotel] made it impossible for me ever again to be taken in by the white man's boast of the superiority of his morals over those of the Negro."

A week into his job, Walter learned he had been hired under the assumption that he was white. Mortified by his unintentional "passing," he decided to resign, but the bell captain talked him out of it. After all, said the captain, Walter had never been asked his race, and he was doing nothing illegal.

Walter remained at the hotel for the rest of the summer, but he was plagued by his accidental deception. When the hotel manager offered him the higher-paying job of clerk the next year, Walter announced that he was black. "You are better educated and better bred than most of my clerks," said the surprised manager. "I'm from New Hampshire, and the fact that you are a Negro makes no difference to me," he added. "But I am operating a hotel in the South and my guests would leave if they found out that you were colored." Walter and the Piedmont parted company.

From such incidents, Walter learned that there were two worlds, one white, one black. The perplexing fact was that he belonged to both. "I am one of the two in the color of my skin," he reflected; "I am the other in my spirit and my heart."

One tumultuous night in September 1906, 13-year-old Walter really learned what it meant to be black in the South. The summer had been oppressively hot, fraying tempers and bringing Atlanta's

A contemporary newspaper illustration shows white Atlantans attacking black citizens during the city's bloody riot of 1906. The September rampage, which followed a sweltering summer and a series of false reports about black crime, took 10 black lives and injured hundreds of others. White later said the riot taught him who he was: "A Negro . . . a person to be hunted, hanged, abused, discriminated against."

Georgia state troopers patrol Atlanta after the 1906 riot. Two nights of violence left 13-year-old Walter White shaken but sure of one thing: "I was glad I was not one of those who hated," he wrote later.

long-simmering racial tensions to the boiling point. Adding fuel to the fire had been the stage production of Thomas Dixon's *The Clansman*, an inflammatory novel that pictured black men as dangerous savages, white women as their prey, and Ku Klux Klan members as heroes.

Further heating up the racial climate was a particularly ugly battle for the Georgia governorship. Although the candidates disagreed on economic policies, they stood together on one major issue: Blacks, who were slowly gaining limited political power, should be removed from politics, preferably by disfranchisement (loss of the right to vote). Taking advantage of the prejudice and fears of many white voters, the candidates proclaimed the end of the white race unless it suppressed the primitive, bloodthirsty black population.

The antiblack campaign gained strength from the *Atlanta Journal*, a newly established newspaper that increased its circulation by printing lurid but untrue stories about black rapists, thieves, and murderers. In a typical editorial, appearing on August 1, 1906, the *Journal* said, "The negro . . . grows more bumptious on the street, more impudent in his dealings with white men, and then, when he cannot achieve social equality as he wishes, with the instinct of the barbarian to destroy what he cannot attain to, he lies in wait . . . and assaults the fair young girlhood of the south."

Georgia's whites, in short, were enveloped in a carefully constructed web of hatred and lies. By the end of the summer, Atlanta was ready to explode.

On Saturday, September 24, Walter White recalled later, he noticed that a peculiar silence seemed to enshroud Atlanta. As he did on most Saturdays, he accompanied his father on his mail route. Before they set out, Madeline White made her husband promise to be home before dark.

When they reached downtown Atlanta, Walter and his father saw groups of white men on every street corner. The clusters grew rapidly; as daylight faded, throngs of men filled the streets. Suddenly, the city echoed with the sound of tramping feet as whites hunted down blacks.

Racing for the safety of their home, the Whites saw a small figure hobbling toward their buggy. It was the local shoeshine man, whose crippled leg slowed his frantic effort to escape a gang of pursuing white men. As Walter and his father looked on in horror, the mob caught up with the defenseless bootblack, then clubbed and kicked him to death. "There goes another nigger," shouted a member of the frenzied mob.

George White searched for an opening in the crowd, but it seemed to multiply out of darkness itself, chasing down every black person in sight and blocking any escape. Ignored by the mob because of their light skin, Walter and his father remained powerless witnesses to the savagery that surrounded them.

When George White and his son were finally able to turn into the city's main street, they saw a carriage barreling toward them at full speed. Three black men clung to its sides while the white driver slashed at its howling pursuers with his buggy whip. As the carriage sped past, it crashed against the Whites' vehicle, jolting its occupants and causing its horse to rear and bolt. Regaining control of the animal, White headed for home. Around the next corner, he saw an elderly black woman fleeing from a band of club-wielding white men.

This time George White saw that he and Walter could be of help: "Father handed the reins to me and, though he was of slight stature, reached down and lifted the woman into the cart," Walter recalled years afterward. "I did not need to be told to lash the mare to the fastest speed she could muster." Their passenger safely aboard, the Whites drove home at full gallop.

The next morning, the hats of black victims hung, like spoils of war, from the telegraph poles of Atlanta. Once again, an ominous silence pervaded the city. During that long day, George White received a tip: A mob was preparing to march on Atlanta's black neighborhood that night, and its path would take it past the Whites' Houston Street home.

White lost no time in preparing for the onslaught. Although he hated the sight of firearms, he gathered guns and ammunition from friends, determined to protect his family and hard-earned home. Darkness fell, but no house on Houston Street showed a light. "Toward midnight," Walter White wrote later, "the unnatural quiet was broken by a roar that grew steadily in volume. Even today I grow tense in remembering it." George White ordered his wife and daughters to barricade themselves in the back of the house while he and Walter guarded the front windows. Ironically, because of its meticulous upkeep, the Whites' house drew the attention of the mob.

"That's where that nigger mail carrier lives!" one of the men shouted. "Let's burn it down! It's too nice for a nigger to live in." Turning to Walter, George White said calmly, "Son, don't shoot until the first man puts his foot on the lawn and then—don't you miss!"

In that instant, Walter White wrote later, "I knew who I was: I was a Negro, a human being with an invisible pigmentation which marked me a person to be hunted, hanged, abused, discriminated against, kept in poverty and ignorance. . . . No matter how low a white man fell, he could always hold fast to the smug conviction that he was superior to two-thirds of the world's population, for those two-thirds were not white."

As the mob surged toward the Whites' house, neighbors fired a volley of shots into the darkness. Alarmed, the whites shifted direction and moved on to look for easier victims. Walter stood by the window, watching the departing crowd and trying to make sense of what he had seen. The night before, he and his father had been safe because they looked white. Now, identified as black, they had been threatened with injury, perhaps death. And yet, Walter would recall, "I knew . . . that my skin was as white as the skin of those who were coming at me." Just what did skin color mean? The question would confront him again and again.

Walter had, however, gained one piece of solid knowledge from the terrifying night: His connection with his racial heritage formed an unbreakable bond. "I was gripped by the knowledge of my identity, and in the depths of my soul I was vaguely aware that I was glad of it," he wrote years afterward. "I was glad I was not one of those who hated."

A Ku Klux Klan unit parades through Atlanta in 1922. Racial tensions would trouble the Georgia capital for decades after the 1906 riot, but the tireless efforts of Walter White and other civil rights leaders finally bore fruit: In the 1960s, Atlanta peacefully integrated its schools, and in 1973, it elected Maynard Jackson, a black attorney, as its mayor.

3
"DECIDE WHAT'S RIGHT AND DON'T FALTER"

WALTER WHITE ENROLLED at Atlanta University in 1912. A star member of the college debating team and a diligent if ineffective football player, he was popular among his fellow students, who elected him president of the class of 1916. In the summer after his junior year, he worked for the Standard Life Insurance Company, selling policies to people in backwoods Georgia. "I could not afford to rent an automobile, or even a horse and buggy," he recalled later. "That summer I walked more miles, usually under a broiling sun, than at any period of my life. But I learned a lot from talking with whites in these rural areas, especially when they believed me to be one of their own race."

In later years, White was often asked how he managed to escape hating white people. He usually credited the men and women, many of them white northerners, who had taught at Atlanta University. These people, he said, could have earned much larger salaries in the North, but "they had been moved by a selfless devotion to a cause in which they

Atlanta University's football squad gathers for a portrait in 1913. Recalling his college years, White (back row, fourth from left) wrote, "In addition to playing not too good football, serving as president of my class, being a member of the debating team, and a few other extracurricular activities of that sort, I worked throughout the school year."

passionately believed—education for the Negro on the same basis as for others."

White said that from these dedicated teachers, he had learned "that not all white people were infected with delusions of racial superiority and opposed to progress for the Negro. It was they who saved me from the defeatist belief that all whites are evil and bigoted in their attitude toward dark-skinned people."

When White graduated from college, Standard Life offered him a clerical job. It paid little, but it would provide good training in a solid business, and he accepted it quickly.

Deciding he looked too young for a budding executive, White decided to grow a mustache, but the effort failed to accomplish its goal: "At its most luxuriant period," he recalled with amusement, "[the mustache] was hardly visible, since it turned out to be a delicate champagne color."

Despite his youthful appearance, White did well at Standard, soon earning a promotion to cashier. His future in the insurance world looked promising. But during his first year with the company, his interests began to move in another direction, sparked by some unsettling news about the Atlanta school system. In 1914, two years earlier, the city's school board had discontinued the eighth grade for black children. To increase its budget for white schools, the board was now proposing to eliminate the seventh grade in black schools.

Atlantans of both races paid the same school-tax rates but equality stopped there. The city's black schools had always been deplorable, even for the South. Ignoring the Supreme Court's *Plessy v. Ferguson* ruling, Atlanta provided black children with separate but unequal elementary schools and with no high schools at all. Now the city threatened to make a bad system even worse by chopping off another year of education.

White and his friends at the insurance company, most of them educated young black men, saw the proposal as a potential disaster: It could mark the beginning of the end for all black public education in Georgia. The young professionals resolved to stand up and fight, although they knew they faced overwhelming odds. Atlanta's blacks formed a minority of the city's population; haunted by the memory of the murderous 1906 riots, they had maintained political silence for years. In all of Atlanta's history, blacks had never joined forces to oppose the wishes of the white majority.

Realizing they would need help, White and his group decided to write to the NAACP, the biracial organization formed in 1909 to promote equality for blacks. Word of this plan somehow reached the Atlanta school board. Astonished and outraged by the blacks' audacity, board members quickly and secretly shifted the date for the meeting at which the seventh-grade elimination proposal was to be decided. Luckily for the black citizens' movement, news of the board's strategy leaked out, and on the day of the vote, the black delegation appeared at the meeting.

Most of the white school board members listened in silent contempt as the "impudent, radical Negro delegation" presented its case. In the form of a lengthy petition largely composed by Walter White, the delegation not only disputed the city's legal right to abandon black seventh grades, but demanded equal schooling, including a high school education for black children.

Surprisingly, a handful of the white board members actually listened to the powerful document; one of them, future Atlanta mayor James L. Key, even endorsed it. "Gentlemen, I want to plead guilty to every word these men have spoken," Key told his startled colleagues. "As long as I am a member of this board I pledge my word here today that I shall fight

A 1916 graduate of Atlanta University, White proudly models his cap and gown. Years later, he praised his college teachers, "the unselfish men and women who had forsaken their homes in New England to go south to teach in schools like Atlanta University." These instructors, said White, "had been moved by a selfless devotion to a cause in which they passionately believed—education for the Negro on the same basis as for others."

for the rights of these men. I shall cast my vote against every move that tries to take away from them what is theirs."

In the end, the school board backed down and agreed to keep the black schools' seventh grades. The decision heartened White and his associates: Inexperienced, few in number, and equipped with little more than determination, they had faced an entrenched, hostile majority and won their point. But they were still a long way from winning their battle for equality.

Although the school board had conceded on the seventh-grade issue, few of its members had altered their fundamental views. Still needing additional money for education, the board voted to issue municipal bonds; revenue from their sale—all of it—would go to the city's white schools.

Aware that this new battle called for heavy artillery, the city's small core of black activists decided to establish an NAACP chapter in Atlanta. They elected 23-year-old Walter White as the unit's secretary and went to work. Although few had any legal experience, they began to study local and state laws, hoping to find a way to prevent the sale of the municipal bonds.

The group soon discovered that a bond issue could be passed only on the approval of two-thirds of the city's registered voters. Few regular voters bothered to cast their ballots on such unexciting questions as municipal finance. Thus the key to victory, reasoned the activists, lay in getting black voters to the polls on voting day. This was a tall order.

Atlanta's black citizens had long been isolated from the decision-making process, kept from the voting booth by a number of carefully designed obstacles. Among the most notorious was the poll tax, a fee required of voters. Although the tax applied to all voting citizens, election officials rarely

An effigy offers a silent warning to would-be black voters. Ignoring such messages, White and his friends organized Atlanta's black community in 1917, producing enough votes to defeat the planned curtailment of black public education in the Georgia capital.

asked for whites' receipts, but almost always made blacks produce theirs.

Further curtailing blacks' right to vote was the Georgia law calling for *cumulative* poll taxes: Before a man was allowed to vote, he had to pay the tax for every year since his 21st birthday—a requirement poor and elderly blacks found impossible to fulfill. (At this point in American history, all voters were men; women gained the right to vote in 1920.)

Resolved to get blacks to the polls, White and his allies canvassed the entire black community, calling at each house and explaining the bond issue and the importance of its defeat. In response, a river of black men marched off to register, poll tax or no poll tax.

One old man, White recalled later, was so determined to vote that he "paid back poll taxes with accrued interest for thirty-two years—a sum he could ill afford—in order to vote, even though all his children were long past grammar or high school age."

When dumbfounded white officials tallied the vote, they discovered they had lost: Black voters had tipped the balance and defeated the bond issue. For the first time, the white community saw that its only hope of getting money for schools lay in negotiations with the black community. After a series of conferences, new funds were allocated for black education, not only to upgrade black elementary schools but to construct a high school for black teenagers.

During its campaign to motivate black voters, the Atlanta chapter of the NAACP had invited the association's national organizer, Field Secretary James Weldon Johnson, to make an address. Black Atlantans streamed into a local movie theater to hear his speech, which awed young Walter White. "There was none of the sonorous, flamboyant oratory of that era in the meeting," White wrote later, "only the quiet, irrefutable presentation of the facts and the need to wipe out race prejudice before the hate thereby engendered destroyed both the victims and the perpetrators."

White, who introduced Johnson to the crowd, remembered his own speech as mere "rabble rousing," an impassioned tirade that ended with Patrick Henry's celebrated demand of 1776, "Give me liberty or give me death!" Overblown or not, White's words stirred the audience—and impressed Johnson.

The New York NAACP official, who saw White as a potential leader, confirmed his high opinion of the young "hot head" after a postspeech dinner with the White family. When he returned to Manhattan, Johnson urged the NAACP board of directors to offer the Atlanta activist a job. With fewer than 9,000

When NAACP executive James Weldon Johnson met White in 1917, he saw not only a 24-year-old "hot head" but a potential leader. Accepting Johnson's offer of a job as assistant NAACP secretary, White began a 38-year career with the historic civil rights organization.

members at that point, the NAACP employed only 3 full-time officials: Field Secretary Johnson, Secretary Royal Freeman Nash, and Publicity and Research Director W. E. B. Du Bois. Johnson suggested White as assistant secretary, and the board agreed.

When the NAACP job offer arrived, White was both amazed and a bit frightened. At 23, he had not yet left his family home, let alone the state of Georgia. And the NAACP job would pay less than he was getting from Standard Life. "To accept," said White, "would mean abandonment of all the plans of financial security I had made." Still, he found the prospect intriguing. A gentle nudge from George White, whose words Walter recorded in his autobiography, finally sent the young man on his way:

> Your mother and I have given you the best education we could afford, and a good Christian home training. . . . Now it is your duty to pass on what you have been given by helping others less fortunate to get a chance in life. I don't want to see you go away. I'll miss you. But remember always, God will be using your heart and brains to do His will. You'll be misunderstood and criticized when you fight so difficult a battle as that created by the race problem. But decide, with the help of God, what's right and don't falter or turn back.

Walter White left for New York a few months later. From then on, he never had time to turn back.

4

LIVES ON THE LINE

WALTER WHITE ARRIVED in New York City on January 31, 1918. After reporting to his boss, NAACP Field Secretary James Weldon Johnson, he took a room in a Harlem boardinghouse and plunged into his new job. Committed to an immense task, and staffed only by part-time volunteers and a handful of salaried employees, the NAACP's Manhattan operation resembled a whirlwind. White's homesickness passed in a flash; his work allowed no time for self-indulgence.

By the time White joined it, the NAACP had been in business for nine years. Founded in 1909, the organization dedicated itself mainly to the suppression of lynching, but it also aimed at securing voting rights for blacks, fostering pride in African-American achievements, and countering racist propaganda. As it gained strength, the NAACP would initiate a strong campaign against segregation in all areas of American life, including education, housing, public transportation, and the armed forces.

White's first year with the NAACP coincided with a vast increase in its membership. During an 8-month recruiting drive in 1918, the organization's rolls jumped from 9,869 to 43,944. By 1920, it would have more than 90,000 members and 8 district conferences, or geographic regions, each with its own officers.

Texans scramble for a better view of the day's entertainment: the 1916 lynching of Jesse Washington, an 18-year-old black accused of killing a white woman. After abducting the mentally retarded teenager, citizens of Waco dragged him to the center of town and, amid shouts and cheers, burned him to death.

Despite the NAACP's intense campaign against lynching, this vicious crime had continued unabated; between 1910 and 1920, almost 900 people died at the hands of self-appointed executioners. Although most lynchings took place in the South, the North claimed its share of victims as well. In 1911, for example, a wounded black man, charged with killing a policeman, had been dragged out of a hospital in Coatesville, Pennsylvania, and burned alive.

Among the South's most mind-numbing murder scenes in this period was one known as the Waco Horror. In the spring of 1916, a mob snatched a mentally retarded black teenager from a Waco, Texas, courtroom, where he awaited trial for killing a white woman. Taken to the town center, the boy was tortured, then tied to a stake. Some 15,000 cheering Texans watched him burn to death.

Americans of today may find it hard to believe that the U.S. government took no action against these appalling crimes, but such was the case. Federal antilynching bills had been introduced from time to time, but none had ever gained presidential support and none had ever overcome the opposition of southern legislators. In 1917, President Woodrow Wilson did issue a public statement urging Americans to help end lynching, but it was a suggestion rather than an impassioned plea. Made only after repeated requests from the NAACP and other concerned citizens, Wilson's statement had no visible effect.

Atrocities like those in Waco and Coatesville naturally terrified most blacks; the savagery, however, made others grimly determined to change things. When Walter White learned of Jim McIlherron's tragic fate, he immediately requested permission to go to Estill Springs. Giving the young assistant secretary his first major assignment, James Johnson told him to go ahead.

After White had tricked McIlherron's killers into revealing the details of the murder, he returned to

White (far left) gathers with NAACP colleagues outside the association's Manhattan headquarters. Standing next to the new assistant secretary is social worker and NAACP cofounder Mary White Ovington; third from the right is educator William Pickens, NAACP field secretary from 1920 to 1942; at far right is NAACP board chairman Joel Spingarn.

New York and published the whole story. Opening new eyes to the unpunished crimes regularly occurring in the United States, his shocking report also recruited more supporters to the antilynching movement.

White involved himself in a broad range of NAACP activities, including the ongoing battle to desegregate schools, hospitals, and housing. Lynchings and race riots, however, soon became his specialty. During the Red Summer of 1919—so called because of its unprecedented number of riots, lynchings, and violent racial confrontations—the NAACP sent White to Chicago, where a particularly bloody series of riots had taken place. During World War I, the industrialized northern cities' need for workers had prompted thousands of southern blacks to relocate. After the war ended in 1918, still more black southerners moved to the Northeast and the Midwest, hoping to find both jobs and racial tolerance. Most found neither. The labor market quickly filled up with returning white soldiers and former war workers, and northern whites proved no more receptive to integration than their southern counterparts.

Although most of Chicago's 1919 rioting—triggered by the efforts of newly arrived blacks to find housing in white neighborhoods—had quieted by the time White arrived, racial hostility continued to smolder. It almost cost White his life. He had assumed, correctly, that his pale skin would protect him from the bands of angry whites who still roamed the streets. He had not, however, considered his own race as a source of danger.

Thus, as White walked through the largely black South Side one evening, he paid no particular attention to a black man half hidden in the shadow of a tree. Suddenly, a shot rang out; White had been perceived as the enemy. He jumped, and the bullet hit a wall inches from his head. From then on, he noted in his autobiography, whenever he ventured into the South Side, he "made sure to have as a companion a Negro who was discernibly a Negro."

In the late summer of 1919, soon after he left Chicago, White headed west again, this time to Phillips County in Arkansas. According to news reports, the county had recently been struck by "black riots." A band of murderous blacks, said the stories, had organized themselves to slaughter whites and had indeed already killed one white man. To preserve order, local law enforcement officers had been forced to kill "a few black revolutionists," and had arrested 79 black men on charges of "murder, insurrection, and a variety of other crimes."

Aware that such reports usually concealed more than they revealed, White's boss, newly appointed

NAACP chief James Weldon Johnson, dispatched his young aide to Arkansas. "I was eager to go to the scene," White recalled. Arming himself with a press card that identified him as a white newspaper reporter, he went to Phillips County. What he found there formed a dramatic contrast to the newspaper reports. Discovering the truth, however, once again placed his life in jeopardy.

In Phillips County, as in much of the South at the time, agriculture relied on sharecropping. Under this system, landowners provided poor farmers with the use of acreage, seed, and tools; in return, the farmers gave the landowners a share of what they raised.

Sharecropping often produced corruption: Unscrupulous landowners frequently lent money to their "croppers" during the lean months of the year. Charging very high interest rates, they forced the farmers into ever-mounting debt, which they could repay only by giving more and more of their crops to the landlord. Unable to save money, the sharecroppers had no way to break out of the system.

The county's black sharecroppers endured the worst of a bad system. For most, the only source of food and other supplies was a landlord-owned store, which sold goods at outrageously high prices. Few landowners felt obliged to account for their prices or for the extra expenses they often tacked onto a farmer's bill. In fact, a black sharecropper risked a beating or worse if he asked for an explanation of his account.

The Constitution's Thirteenth Amendment abolished slavery, and federal law expressly prohibited peonage (the use of laborers bound by debt). Phillips County landowners, however, had been freely practicing peonage and near-slavery for decades. Aware of their rights and desperate to improve their wretched lot, a group of black Phillips County sharecroppers banded together in 1919.

Chicago policemen and bystanders inspect the body of a black man killed during the 1919 Chicago riot, one of the many bloody events that punctuated that year's "Red Summer." In Chicago to investigate the violence, the fair-skinned White almost lost his life to a black gunman who mistook him for a white opponent.

The sharecroppers pooled what little money they had, hired two sympathetic white attorneys, and incorporated themselves as the Progressive Farmers and Household Union of America. Through their association, the farmers hoped to bring cases of tenant abuse before the courts, expose the illegal practices of the landlords, and put an end to their exploitation.

The union's first meeting, held in a small country church, drew dozens of anxious sharecroppers and their wives. The first speaker had just climbed to the pulpit when a hail of bullets tore into the church. As the panicked crowd scrambled for safety, their unseen attackers kept firing, killing and wounding a number of women and men. Knowing of the landowners' fierce opposition to their union, a few of the sharecroppers had brought guns to the meeting. They returned their assailants' fire, mortally wounding one of the white gunmen.

News of the episode flashed through the county, but it had become a different story: Rampaging blacks had murdered an innocent white man. Within the hour, armed white mobs swept the countryside, systematically slaughtering every black man, woman, and child they could find. Although the exact total will never be known, the massacre claimed the lives of at least 200 blacks.

Survivors who failed to escape into the swamps and woods were rounded up like cattle and subjected to trial by mob. "Good niggers"—those who had not joined the farmers' union and who agreed to provide their landlords with a period of free labor—were released. Terrified, most of the captured blacks agreed to their captors' terms. But 79 men refused.

Promptly indicted for murder and insurrection, these stubborn holdouts went to trial five days later. After a speedy hearing, 12 of the 79 received the death sentence, and 67 were given life sentences or

Residents of Phillips County, Arkansas, form posses to hunt blacks in the late summer of 1919. After a white man died during a raid on a black sharecroppers' meeting, white mobs tracked down and killed every black person they could find.

20-year prison terms. It was at this point that Walter White arrived on the scene.

Posing as a reporter from a Chicago newspaper, White met with Arkansas governor Charles H. Brough. The governor, clearly not a friend to the black cause, railed about "the foul lies" spread by the "infamous" NAACP "about the good white people of Arkansas." But White acted his part well. When he left the interview, he carried a key to Phillips County: a letter of introduction from the governor describing him as "one of the most brilliant newspapermen" he had ever met.

The letter opened doors all over the county. After gathering data from lawmen, witnesses, and local officials, White spoke to a number of blacks familar with the situation. Finally, he headed for the county jail, where the sheriff had promised him an interview with the convicted men. On his way, a black man passed him and, in an urgent whisper, urged White to follow him into the nearby woods.

"I don't know what you are down here for," the man said to White, "but I just heard them talking

A black sharecropper, victim of the mobs rampaging through the Arkansas countryside in 1919, lies dead at his cabin steps. Posing as a northern newspaper reporter, White uncovered the truth about the massacre, but when local vigilantes discovered his racial identity, he narrowly escaped death himself.

about you—I mean the white folks—and they say they are going to get you. The way I figured it out is that if the white folks are so against you, you must be a friend of ours."

Realizing that his identity had been discovered and that an ambush awaited him, White fled. He took off down the railroad tracks, arrived at the station just as a train was pulling out, and jumped aboard. Shaken and breathless, he managed to convince an inquisitive conductor he had urgent business in Memphis and had not had time to buy a ticket. "But you're leaving, mister, just when the fun is going to start," said the trainman. "There's a damned yellow nigger down here passing for white and the boys are going to get him."

"What'll they do with him?" asked White.

"When they get through with him," said the grinning conductor, "he won't pass for white no more!"

White's account of the Phillips County Massacre, published in the *Chicago Daily News*, brought an unexpected response from the public. Letters of support and donations of money streamed into NAACP headquarters. Aware that they had no hope of appealing the Arkansas convictions in state courts, White and his colleagues turned to the federal court. After a 4-year battle, during which Arkansas 3 times erected gallows for the 12 condemned blacks, the NAACP gained a hearing from the United States Supreme Court.

Arguing the case for the NAACP, prominent white attorney Moorfield Storey asserted that because the Arkansas trial had been dominated by a mob, the accused men had been denied their constitutional right of due process of law. An American, insisted Storey, is a citizen of both a state and the nation, and the state and federal courts share the responsibility of guarding that citizen's constitutional rights.

White and his associates marveled at Storey's brilliant appeal, but they had little hope that the Court would agree. Thus, it was to their delighted astonishment when, on February 19, 1923, the Court reversed the convictions of all 79 men in the Phillips County case. After "more than five years of struggle against unbelievable odds," exulted White, "we had won!"

An avalanche of congratulatory telegrams and letters poured into the NAACP office, but none, recalled White, "was as welcome as a letter written on inexpensive paper in pencil and signed by those of the defendants who were literate enough to write, expressing their gratitude."

Although White was heartened by the outcome of the Arkansas case, he was long haunted by the vision of the "several days and nights of slaughter" that had stained the rolling fields of Phillips County. Between his often grim assignments, however, he lived a stimulating and often exciting personal life: "These early years," he noted in his autobiography, "were not all devoted to work and tragedies."

In 1922, between the outset and the conclusion of the events in Arkansas, White made a request he had been considering for some time: He asked NAACP aide Leah Gladys Powell to marry him. Powell, recalled White, "for two years previous to that had been (from my point of view at least) much the most interesting member of the NAACP staff." White found Gladys (as she preferred to be called) Powell "interesting" because they shared the same work and the same passionate convictions about social justice and equality. His opinion may also have been affected by Powell's stunning good looks.

Powell and her twin sister, Madrenne, recalled a New Yorker who met them at a party, "were the most beautiful women I had ever seen—identical twins with glorious deep bronze complexions. . . . They were breathtaking. It was impossible to look at anyone else."

Soon after his marriage, White reported in his autobiography, "I almost succeeded in becoming a member of the Ku Klux Klan." Triggering this unlikely event was White's receipt of a Klan recruitment letter, boasting of the organization's "valiant services in behalf of white supremacy." White scanned the letter in fascination, realizing how its cunning appeal to patriotism could seduce uneducated, frustrated whites.

America's need for the Klan, said the letter, "when fourteen million people of the colored race are organizing, and when the Anarchist and Bolshevik forces are encroaching daily upon the basic principles of Americanism, cannot fail to be apparent to the thinking man." The missive was signed by one Edward Young Clarke.

White responded to the letter at once, giving a truthful account of himself, but naturally not mentioning his race or affiliation with the NAACP. Thus began an extensive correspondence between White and the Imperial Palace of the Klan. Apparently impressed by White's pretended enthusiasm for the Klan, Clarke eventually asked if he would like to become its New York State organizer. White avoided giving a direct answer, meanwhile gathering valuable inside information about the Klan's recruitment practices and its illegal conspiracy against blacks, Jews, Catholics, and "foreigners." He passed this information on to local and federal law enforcement agencies.

After making an investigation of his own, Clarke realized he had been dealing with the enemy. The friendly correspondence halted, and a barrage of anonymous threats began. Finally, a newsman reported that Klan leaders were telling their members that "a Negro named Walter White" had stolen Klan secrets and must be stopped at any cost.

The New York City Police Department immediately put Walter and Gladys White under protective surveillance; in Atlanta, the police assigned guards to the home of the senior Whites. "Whether it was due to that protection or the cowardice of the Klan I never knew," White said, "but fortunately [my family was] not molested and neither was I."

By now accustomed to danger, White forgot about the Klan's death threats and continued his investigative work. In between his frequent out-of-town trips, he and his wife enjoyed a rich social and intellectual life in New York, a particularly exciting place to be at the time. White's arrival in Manhattan had coincided with the Harlem Renaissance, a cultural phenomenon that produced an extraordinary outpouring of black art and literature.

During the 1920s, Harlem attracted the nation's most gifted black writers, sculptors, painters, and performers; in a short and uniquely fertile period, these creative people made an indelible mark on their nation's artistic history, reawakened blacks' pride in their heritage, and focused national attention on the African-American experience.

Among the many dazzling stars of the Harlem Renaissance were novelists Zora Neale Hurston, Jean Toomer, and Jessie Fauset; poets Langston Hughes, Countee Cullen, and Claude McKay; artists Aaron Douglas and Archibald Motley; and composer-dramatist Hall Johnson. Adding luster to this distinguished company would be Walter White, battler for black justice—and distinguished novelist, essayist, and historian.

5

"AMONG THE HUNTED"

IN 1922, WALTER WHITE said in his autobiography, "Two things happened to me which have been important factors in everything which has followed." The first of these major events was his marriage to Gladys Powell. The second was his introduction to H. L. Mencken.

Henry Louis Mencken, sometimes called the Sage of Baltimore, was one of the era's most influential journalists, authors, and social critics. Americans across the country read Mencken's syndicated *Baltimore Evening Sun* column, relied on his pungent literary criticism, and quoted his classic work, *The American Language*.

White met Mencken through his friend and boss, James Weldon Johnson. The NAACP chief had taken White under his wing from the first, giving him what the younger man called "a liberal education in contemporary literature." Johnson, recalled White, "either purchased for me or recommended my buying books of fiction, poetry, and history and discussion of social problems which he thought would be of permanent value."

A better mentor would have been hard to find. A lawyer, former diplomat, songwriter, magazine editor, poet, and novelist (*The Autobiography of an Ex-Colored Man*; 1912) as well as a social activist, the

White shares a quiet moment with his friend and boss, James Weldon Johnson, in the early 1920s. The multitalented Johnson— diplomat, editor, poet, songwriter, playwright, novelist, and NAACP chief for a decade—helped guide White through his first years in New York City.

Introduced to White in 1922, author and editor Henry Louis Mencken immediately spotted the young man as a prospective writer. Thanks to Mencken's demanding encouragement, White produced his first book, the best-selling novel The Fire in the Flint, *in 1924.*

formidable Johnson seemed to know everyone—and to want to share them with his protégé. In the spring of 1922, he invited White to accompany him on a visit to Mencken, then editor of the popular magazine *The Smart Set.*

Mencken and White liked each other from the start. Soon after their first meeting, the Baltimorean sent the young New Yorker a new book—a novel about blacks written by a white—and asked for his opinion. Highly flattered, White responded with a long, critical letter; the novelist, he said, had "written from the outside looking in," and "fell down badly in his portrayal of what educated Negroes think and feel."

Mencken, always on the lookout for new literary talent, had gotten just the response he had hoped for. "Why don't you do the right kind of novel?" he asked White. "You could do it, and it would create a sensation."

White, who said he had "never even thought about attempting to write fiction," called the suggestion "preposterous." But Mencken, assisted by James Johnson, kept on the case. "They both tried to convince me," White recalled, "that the variety of experiences which my appearance made possible, by permitting me to talk with white people as a white man and with my own people as a Negro, gave me a unique vantage point."

White started the project with "no clearly thought-out plot." But to his surprise, he discovered that as he began to write, "the characters seemed to rise up begging to be described, and creating their own story." By the end the summer, he had completed *The Fire in the Flint*; its title, White explained, was drawn from an old English proverb: "The fire in the flint never shows until it is struck." The novel tells the story of Kenneth Harper, a black, Georgia-born, northern-educated doctor who returns to his hometown to practice medicine and improve the lot of the black population.

Clearly the best physician in the area, Harper is called upon to operate on the daughter of the town's leading white citizen. Although he saves the girl's life, his work among the blacks has incurred the fury of the local landowners and the Ku Klux Klan; in the end, he is lynched.

Although the book "ends in personal tragedy and death for the hero," said White, "one senses that the spirit of revolt against bigotry which he symbolizes will be accelerated rather than diminished by his death."

The merits of *The Fire in the Flint*, most modern critics agree, lie in its message rather than in its literary polish. A furious attack on racism, the book lacks both subtlety and shading. Sinclair Lewis, one of the period's most celebrated novelists (*Main Street*), called *Fire* "splendidly courageous, rather terrifying, and of the highest significance." In a private letter to White, however, Lewis said that while he "rejoiced immensely" in the book, he found it heavy-handed in its depictions of heroes as "faultless" and villains as "fiends."

White had to agree. The "weakness" in his novel, he admitted to Lewis, was one he had often "preached against" when advising young black writers: He had overlooked the fact that "all white men are not super devils nor all Negroes super angels."

Appearing in 1924, *Fire* produced rave reviews in the North ("significant . . . worthwhile . . . few novels have been needed more," said the *New York World*) and outraged denunciations in the South ("the worst libel we have seen on the South and southern men and women," said Georgia's *Savannah Press*). The controversy worked in the book's favor, catapulting it to the top of the best-seller lists in the United States, Europe, and Japan.

Understandably gratified by the book's success—"far beyond its literary merits," insisted its author—White was especially proud of its reception in Germany, where, he noted, "it received the honor of being one of the books burned" after dictator Adolf Hitler and his Nazi party came to power.

Best-selling novelist or not, White kept up his rigorous schedule of NAACP activities, traveling many thousands of miles each year. Among his responsibilities was making speeches, an art at which he excelled. Addressing a variety of audiences, from local school boards to college students to business leaders, White called attention to the nation's racial problems and raised much-needed funds for the NAACP. "His personal charm and wit," noted one observer, "made him popular wherever he spoke."

Even more crucial than his speeches were White's ongoing investigations into racial injustice. In the fall of 1926, for example, he traveled to Aiken, South Carolina, site of an especially shocking quadruple murder. The case had begun the previous spring, when Aiken County sheriff H. H. Howard and three deputies paid a call on the Lowmans, a local black family suspected of selling illegal liquor.

Startled by the sudden appearance of four armed, nonuniformed white men in their yard, Annie Lowman and her 27-year-old daughter, Bertha, ran for their front door. The sheriff caught Bertha and punched her in the mouth. When Annie Lowman raced to her daughter's aid, a deputy shot the 55-year-old woman dead. Hearing the gunfire, 22-year-old Demon Lowman and his cousin Clarence, 15, rushed in from the field where they were working. A bout of wild shooting followed; minutes later, the three Lowmans had been critically wounded and Sheriff Howard lay dead.

The county treated the Lowmans' injuries, then tried them for murder. Although the three deputies swore that none of the blacks could have shot the sheriff, the young men were sentenced to death, Bertha Lowman to life in prison. Not even in the South of 1926, however, could such a mockery of justice go unnoticed; the South Carolina Supreme Court ordered a new trial. Before it could take place, a mob of whites dragged the Lowmans out of jail, threw them into a truck, and drove them to a tourist camp outside Aiken.

As 2,000 white women and men looked on, the Lowmans were released from their bonds, told to run, then cut down by a hail of bullets. The mob, according to one report, "laughed loudly at the clever joke." When they realized they had not quite finished off Bertha Lowman, the gunmen advanced on her writhing body. "We had to waste more than 50 bullets on the wench," a grinning participant reported later, "before one of them stopped her howling."

After looking into the events of October 8, an Aiken County coroner's jury issued its report: "Death at the hands of parties unknown."

Risking his own life at every moment, Walter White conducted a thorough investigation of the lynching. The Lowmans' white lawyer gave him much useful information, then offered to introduce him to another white man who could tell him even more. After the lawyer dropped him at the man's home, White awaited his host, feeling relaxed for the first time in days. But suddenly every nerve came alive. "There appeared in the doorway a figure dressed in the full regalia of the Ku Klux Klan," he recalled in his autobiography. "I thought that I had walked into a trap."

The robed man then removed his hood and revealed himself as White's host. Pointing to his Klan outfit, he said, "I show you this so that you will realize I know what I am talking about."

Novelist Sinclair Lewis publicly praised The Fire in the Flint; *addressing White privately, however, he criticized the book's rather crudely drawn characters and its "tendency to propagandize." White, he said, "must learn to be more just to his villains" and "remember that fiendish things are often done by men who are not essentially fiends."*

Ku Klux Klan members attend a Chicago church service in the mid-1920s. Temporarily quiet after the 1870s, the Klan roared back to life in 1915; by 1924, its peak year, at least 4.5 million "white male persons, native-born Gentile citizens," as they defined themselves, had joined the group of hooded terrorists. Klan tactics, used against Jews and Roman Catholics as well as blacks, included whipping, tarring and feathering, branding, mutilating, and lynching.

As White recovered his composure, the man unfolded his story. He had joined the Klan, he said, under the impression that it was a civic organization, aimed at cleaning up local politics and reducing crime. He resigned as soon as he recognized his mistake, but he had lived in fear of his life ever since. Leading White into the next room, he displayed the imposing array of guns he had collected to defend himself and his family against Klan revenge.

Looking at the man's arsenal, White recalled, reawoke "the sense of terror which I had known that night in 1906 when my father and I, guns in hand, had knelt in the dark at a window of our house in Atlanta." He added that "although everything in me hated everything connected with the Ku Klux Klan, I could not help feeling . . . a bond of sympathy between this ex-Kluxer and myself. We both knew what it was to be among the hunted."

The former Klansman confirmed and enlarged the lawyer's information about the lynching and its perpetrators: Klan members all, they were part of Aiken's elite. White obtained signed affidavits that the Klan had masterminded the lynching and that the lynch mob had included the new sheriff and his deputies, the jailer, a member of the state legislature, three relatives of the governor, and many of the county's prominent business, political, and social leaders.

White's report on the Aiken murders created a national sensation and prompted South Carolina's governor to order a grand jury investigation of the case. By now, even normally conservative southern newspapers called for justice. The Columbia, South Carolina, *Record* called the matter "the most important case . . . that any Grand Jury in South Carolina has had to consider within the past 20 years." On the grand jury's decision, said the newspaper, "depends the honor, not alone of Aiken County, but of the whole people of South Carolina."

Judge J. Henry Johnson went even further. Calling the lynchings "deliberate, wilful, cowardly murder," he told jury members that "the time for words is past. It is time for action. Say you propose to bring them to justice or say you don't propose to do anything. And God help Aiken County and South Carolina if you fail to do something."

But the grand jury did fail. Reporting its inability to reach a decision after three attempts, its members requested and received dismissal. The case was closed. Nevertheless, White's revelations had focused the attention of millions of Americans on the Ku Klux Klan and its reign of terror. By revealing the lynchers' identities, White had begun to light up the shadows that had long shielded such criminals. The march toward racial justice moved with agonizing slowness, but thanks to White and other dedicated crusaders, it was moving.

6

"DIFFICULT DAYS"

SOON AFTER HE completed his investigation of the Lowman massacre, White published his second—and last—work of fiction. Encouraged by the success of *The Fire in the Flint*, he had been working on the new novel on and off for two years. This one, entitled *Flight*, examines the development of Mimi Daquin, a young, light-skinned black southerner, as she undergoes a series of crises in which she must confront her black heritage.

The novel deals with the issue of blacks passing for white; Daquin, who lives first as a black, then as a white, finally comes to embrace her racial identity instead of fleeing it. White infused *Flight* with images from his own childhood. In one scene, for example, Daquin and her father witness the murder of a black man by a white mob, echoing White's memories of the 1906 Atlanta riots. "The death before her very eyes of that unknown man," White writes of Daquin, "shook from her all the apathy of the past. There flashed through her mind in letters that seared her brain, 'I too am a Negro!' "

In writing *Flight*, White heeded the criticisms of Sinclair Lewis and others, deliberately toning down his melodramatic tendencies. Far subtler than its predecessor, this second novel also turned out to be

By 1929, White was the author of two successful novels and a widely acclaimed study of lynching, Rope and Faggot: A Biography of Judge Lynch. *The 1929 work, observed one critic, "makes it unnecessary for any other book on the subject to be written for many years to come."*

far less popular, failing to reach the huge audience that had gobbled up the sensationalistic *Fire in the Flint*. Praised for its improved style but criticized for its lack of drama, *Flight* achieved only modest sales.

But if *Flight* earned its author disappointing royalties, it put him into position to write another, more important book. Soon after the publication of *Flight*, the Guggenheim Foundation, an organization that awarded cash fellowships to creative Americans, indicated its interest in White. Pleased by the prospect of receiving $2,500—enough to support his family for a whole year in an inexpensive European country—White gave foundation officials a list of references. One of them, Sinclair Lewis, responded with special enthusiasm.

"It seems to me," Lewis wrote, "that Walter F. White is ideally the type of person, and that his work is ideally the kind of work, which the Guggenheim Foundation desires to assist. . . . He has a sense of drama; [his work has] a feeling of dignity and importance; he has sharp observation and an admirable sense of words."

White jokingly complained that Lewis's praise gave him a swelled head. "Good Lord, man, I ought to charge you for a new hat!" he wrote his friend. "Honesty compels me to say that you were too laudatory but the same affliction causes me to say that I am damned glad you were and I shall be ever grateful to you whether I get the fellowship or not."

As it happened, he did get it. His mission: to write "a three-generation novel of Negro life." White, his pregnant wife, and their toddler daughter, Jane, sailed for France in July 1927. Through friends, the Whites found a splendid 8-room house in southern France; because its rent was only $250 per year, White knew he could stretch the foundation money to support his family—which soon included Walter, Jr.,—in comfort.

White had thought that by distancing himself from what he called "the daily fare of lynching and injustice with which the NAACP constantly dealt," he could relax and write a leisurely novel. Instead, he discovered that distance "seemed to accentuate rather than diminish concern with what was happening back home to those who could do so little to help themselves."

He soon found himself furiously writing not a novel but, as he put it, "a study of the complex influences—economic, political, social, religious, sexual—behind the gruesome, and too little understood, phenomenon of lynching." Entitled *Rope and Faggot: A Biography of Judge Lynch*, the book explored the history of lynching; in it, White included many of his own experiences as an NAACP investigator. ("Judge" Charles Lynch, an 18th-century Virginia planter, presided over an extralegal court during the disordered days of the American Revolution. Although Lynch was said to be a just man who rarely issued death sentences, his name attached itself to all extralegal executions.)

Published in 1929, *Rope and Faggot* would earn some criticism for its alleged lack of "scientific detachment," but most readers praised the insights it offered into a barbaric tradition. "Mr. White's book on lynching," wrote one observer, "supersedes all other publications on this topic and makes it unnecessary for any other book on the subject to be written for many years to come."

Soon after the publication of *Rope and Faggot*, NAACP director James Weldon Johnson took a one-year leave of absence to write a book himself. "I blithely accepted the responsibility of acting secretary," recalled White, "wholly unaware of the difficult days immediately ahead."

Those "difficult days" began with the October 1929 stock market crash, an economic catastrophe

that quickly plunged the nation into the worst depression in its history. Thousands of businesses and factories closed their doors, throwing millions of men and women out of work. Hardest hit were blacks, who had just begun to enter the economic mainstream. "The grim years were upon us," recalled White, "and interracial tensions began to mount too."

Along with many other blacks, White felt especially bitter about President Herbert Hoover's Republican administration and its apparent lack of concern for the plight of minorities. Hoover, said White, "sat stolidly in the White House, refusing bluntly to receive Negro citizens who wished to lay before him the facts of their steadily worsening plight or to consider any remedial legislation or governmental action. His attitude to Negroes caused me to coin a phrase which gained considerable currency, particu-

Evicted from the Missouri land they had farmed for generations, black sharecroppers prepare to load up their belongings and move on. The Great Depression of the 1930s uprooted thousands of Americans of all races, but blacks, usually at the bottom of the economic ladder, suffered most.

larly in the Negro world, in which I described Hoover as 'the man in the lily-White House.' "

White got his first chance to do battle with Hoover in 1930. To fill a new vacancy in the nine-member Supreme Court, the nation's highest judicial body, Hoover nominated John J. Parker, a U.S. circuit court judge from North Carolina. Neither White nor most other Americans knew much about Parker, but his southern background raised a warning flag. White began an immediate investigation of the judge's record.

He soon discovered that although Parker had made few noteworthy decisions in his time on the federal bench, he had made his position on black rights more than clear. An unsuccessful Republican candidate for the North Carolina governorship in 1920, Parker had called for an end to black voting rights. "The participation of the Negro in politics,"

Arthur B. Spingarn (left), honorary president of the NAACP, confers with White during their successful 1930 campaign against Supreme Court nominee John J. Parker. White's opposition to Judge Parker stemmed from the jurist's attitude toward blacks: "The participation of the Negro in politics," Parker had said, "is a source of evil and danger."

he had said, "is a source of evil and danger to both races and is not desired by the wise men in either race or by the Republican party of North Carolina."

"Plainly," observed White with characteristic understatement, "this attitude would constitute a grave threat to the future of the Negro." He sent Parker a telegram, asking if he had indeed made the statement about blacks, and if so, if he still held such beliefs. When Parker failed to respond, White and the NAACP board of directors reached a decision: The organization would "protest and oppose as vigorously as possible Judge Parker's confirmation." (Supreme Court justices, who hold their post for life, are nominated by the president but must be confirmed by the Senate.)

On behalf of the NAACP, White formally asked Hoover to withdraw Parker's nomination. As expected, the president refused. White's next move was to appear before the Senate committee considering the nomination. When he spoke, White recalled later, several southern senators appeared outraged by the gall "of a Negro organization presuming to voice an opinion on a nomination to the Supreme Court."

Hoping to embarrass White, the contemptuous legislators peppered him with complicated legal questions. White, however, refused to be drawn into such a trap. He confined his testimony to the fact that Parker had "advocated the disfranchisement of Negro American citizens" even though the Constitution's Fourteenth and Fifteenth Amendments guaranteed blacks the right to vote.

Did Mr. White not know, Senator Lee Overman of North Carolina asked scathingly, that "niggras vote freely throughout North Carolina?" No, replied White coolly, he did not know this, and neither did the senator; there was, in fact, "ample proof to the contrary."

White had stated his case well, but he knew his words had fallen on deaf ears. His next move was to bring the issue to the public. Dispatching NAACP officials to cities around the nation and calling all the organization's regional branches into action, White set up a massive campaign to inform black voters about Parker and the threat he posed to them. The NAACP urged black voters and black church, fraternal, labor, and educational groups to contact their senators, urging them to oppose Parker. The results astonished even the optimistic White.

"At first a trickle, the telegrams, letters, petitions, long distance telephone calls, and personal visits to senators in Washington grew to an avalanche," he reported jubilantly. "Senators who at first had been apathetic or contemptuous began to pay attention to the unprecedented articulateness of Negroes."

Still, support for Parker continued strong. His supporters warned senators that the judge's defeat would serve as a precedent for future Supreme Court nominations. No future president, warned one Georgia newspaper, would dare to nominate a Court justice whose views were not "entirely satisfactory to the National Association for the Advancement of Colored People [and] Walter White." The Parker battle became a hot topic, filling the editorial pages of the nation's newspapers and triggering debates among public officials, columnists, news analysts, and private citizens.

On May 7, 1930, the day of the Senate vote, no one—not the reporters, not the spectators packed into the Senate gallery, not the senators themselves—was sure of the outcome. Many senators had assured White that they would vote against Parker, but as he listened in dismay, several went back on their word during the roll call of votes.

After a lengthy, spirited, and sometimes ugly debate, the senators voted, and the clerk rose to announce the results. White held his breath. Parker's confirmation would deliver a crushing blow to the thousands of blacks who had rallied together to make their voice heard. The presence of this self-professed racist on the country's highest court would suggest a denial of the presence of blacks in American life.

"For confirmation—39," read the clerk. "Against confirmation—41." White breathed a monumental sigh of relief. "The shift of one vote to create a tie," he noted, "would have been a disaster." (According to the Constitution, a tie vote in the Senate is resolved by the vice-president. Hoover's vice-president, Charles Curtis, would naturally have voted to confirm Parker.) Black America had spoken, and its voice had been heard, loud and clear.

Black voters had made it plain that they would not cast their ballots for the senators who supported Parker. "Those threats," said White, "had to be implemented or else Negro voters would be laughed at the next time they appealed to their elected representatives." Accordingly, the NAACP once again departed from its usually nonpolitical stance.

The next issue of *The Crisis*, the NAACP's official publication, listed the senators who had voted for Parker; these legislators, noted the paper, "have Negro constituents in . . . large numbers, and against

Peaceful demonstrators march through the nation's capital with flags and signs: "Is this civilization?" asks one. Another reads, "Congress discusses constitutionality while the smoke of human bodies darkens the heavens." Despite innumerable such protests against lynching, and despite White's tireless battle for antilynching legislation, Congress never outlawed the barbaric practice.

the expressed wishes of these constituents, they voted for the confirmation of Judge Parker. . . . Paste this in your hat and keep it there." Two of these senators met defeat the following November, and eight others lost their seat over the next two years. The Parker episode, White observed with satisfaction, marked "the political coming of age of the hitherto-ignored Negro voters."

Soon after the election, James Weldon Johnson announced that his doctors had forbidden him to resume his heavy work load as NAACP chief. The organization's board immediately named acting secretary White as Johnson's successor. Accepting the job—but wondering "what troubles lay ahead"—White continued his campaign for black civil rights. At the top of his agenda was the securing of federal laws against lynching, against the disfranchisement of blacks, and against the unequal spending of tax money for schools and other public facilities.

These goals meant spending increasing time in Washington, D.C. "What I saw and heard there," White recalled in his autobiography, "[placed] a severe tax on my faith in the democratic process." Week after week, he put in 18-hour days of what he called "frustration and double-dealing at the hands of congressmen and senators who were trying to evade ironclad promises." After one particularly maddening day, White wrote his wife. "Democracy," he said, "must be tough-fibred to survive practice of it by democrats."

Evoking such temporary bitterness were deeply disturbing but typical days like one White spent in the House of Representatives. He was seated in the gallery, listening to southern lawmakers orate about "states' rights" and the needlessness of antilynching legislation, when a reporter friend summoned him outside. Grimly, the newspaperman handed White a news bulletin: Two black man had just been lynched by blowtorch in Mississippi. "It was," wrote the shaken White, "one of the most unbelievable barbarities in human history."

White sent the clipping to the New York congressman who was leading the fight for the antilynching bill. In a quiet voice, the congressman read the dispatch. "One would have thought that such a revelation would have silenced, at least temporarily, the congressional defenders of lynching," White wrote later. "It did not. After the gasp of horror which swept the House had subsided, the southern orators resumed their onslaught as though nothing had happened."

Soon afterward, White experienced another disheartening encounter, this one with a fellow lobbyist (an individual who tries to influence legislators on behalf of a special-interest group). Approaching him outside the Senate chamber, this "high-salaried, assertive representative," recalled White, "bit off the

White, his five sisters, and his brother, George (at rear), join their parents in 1930 for a last full-family portrait. One year later, George White, Sr., died in an Atlanta hospital's squalid "colored ward," leaving his son Walter filled with grief, rage, and a strong sense of responsibility: "It's up to you," George told Walter, "to make love as positive an emotion in the world as are prejudice and hate."

end of a cigar and spat it out on the immaculate tile floor."

"I have been watching you a long time," said the cigar biter. He then assured White that he had absolutely no chance of getting an antilynching bill passed unless he changed his tactics. Instead of appealing to the "better nature" of politicans, said the man, White should "get something" on them and threaten to expose it. "I am going to help you pass your antilynching bill by letting you have what we have dug up," he added expansively.

Somewhat bewildered, White agreed to meet the lobbyist in his office. There, his would-be benefactor produced thick folders on every member of the Senate. Each file, recalled White, contained stacks of data, most of it obviously false, implicating the senators in acts that "might well make a normal human being afraid to sit [in] the United States Senate."

White glanced through a few of the files, then "felt an overwhelming urge to wash [his] hands with carbolic acid soap." As politely as he could, he declined the lobbyist's offer of help. "He looked at me," recalled White, "as though I were mentally deranged."

"It won't cost you a penny," said the astonished lobbyist. "You'd be a fool not to use it!" Rising to leave, White explained that he and the NAACP were fighting for a principle, and that they would never use such a method to achieve their goals. "To this day," White recalled with some amusement, "he looks at me whenever I encounter him as though he is now convinced that Negroes have no brains."

Not long after dealing with the "helpful" lobbyist, White faced another case of racial discrimination, this one a personal tragedy. One day in 1931, he received an urgent call from Atlanta: His 70-year-old father, George, had been struck by a car and seriously injured. White rushed to his hometown, where he found his father in the city hospital's dilapidated "Negro ward."

White's brother-in-law, Eugene Martin, told him the story. George White had been crossing an Atlanta street when a recklessly speeding automobile had careened into him. The driver had lifted the unconscious, light-skinned man into his car and taken him to the white emergency room at Grady Hospital. There, doctors worked frantically to save the elderly man. When he learned of the accident, Martin raced to Grady but found no trace of George White in the "colored" ward.

Checking with the hospital's white section, he discovered that a man of his father-in-law's description was then in the emergency room. "Do you know who this man is?" asked a hospital official.

"Yes," said the brown-skinned Martin. "He is my father-in-law."

The official's eyes widened. "Have we put a nigger in the white ward?" he asked in horror.

"Father was snatched from the examination table lest he contaminate the 'white' air, and taken hurriedly across the street in a driving downpour of rain to the 'Negro' ward," recounted Walter White. He spent the next two weeks at his father's bedside, watching helplessly as the critically injured man grew steadily weaker.

Unlike its gleaming, splendidly equipped white counterpart, the hospital's black section was dark, damp, overcrowded, and understaffed. Cockroaches —their presence "occasionally varied by the appearance of a rat," recalled Walter White—roamed its peeling walls and sticky floors. The facility's handful of black doctors and nurses did their best, White said, but they could provide only minimal care for the patients who packed the wards.

Two weeks after the accident, a band of white men and women came to the black ward to sing hymns. "Maybe [I] should have been grateful that they crossed the color line to sing for the black people, too," White wrote later. "But I wasn't. I yelled at them. I told them to go away—for God's sake, to go away. And let my father die in peace. And then father died."

George White had "never broken a law in his life—not even a small one," said his son. "They let him die like a criminal—like an outcast—like an animal." At that point, Walter White said, "I hated all white people. . . . I hated the sight of my own white face in the mirror." In time, though, White said he regained his balance by thinking about his father's last words of advice:

"Human kindness, decency, love, whatever you wish to call it, is the only real thing in the world," George White had told his son. "It's up to you . . . and others like you, to use your education and talents in an effort to make love as positive an emotion in the world as are prejudice and hate. That's the only way the world can save itself. Don't forget that."

"I have remembered," wrote Walter White.

7

CAPITAL GAINS

WALTER WHITE IS "a great nuisance," said Eleanor Roosevelt to a friend. "However," added the wife of America's 32nd president, "if I were colored, I think I should have about the same obsession that he has."

Elected to the presidency in 1932, Franklin Delano Roosevelt inherited the worst economic depression in his nation's 156-year history. The Great Depression, triggered by the collapse of the stock market in 1929, struck Americans of all races and classes. Hardest hit, however, were blacks. One of every four white workers lost his or her job; among blacks, the figure was one of every two.

Producing hatred as well as fear, the depression stirred some people to look for a scapegoat—a group upon whom the trouble could be blamed. The lynching of blacks, on the downturn for some years, began to increase. Southern lynch mobs killed 8 blacks in 1929; in 1930, the officially recorded total—probably far lower than the actual number—jumped to 24. "Intense anti-Negro feeling has the states of the cotton belt in its grip," observed the

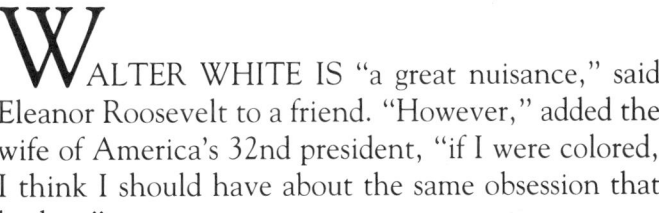

In one of his many appearances before the Senate Judiciary Subcommittee, White testifies on a federal antilynching bill. Despite his extraordinary powers of persuasion, White never swayed the "southern bloc," which routinely torpedoed every antilynching bill introduced. One South Carolina senator even called lynching a necessary weapon to "protect the fair womanhood of the South from beasts."

magazine *Outlook* in late 1930, "and every few days it strikes down a victim."

Fearful whites also attacked blacks on the economic front. The Illinois Central Railroad, for example, hired a group of black firemen in the early 1930s; within a few months, white railroad workers had murdered seven of the firemen and seriously injured another eight. Armed whites routinely invaded meetings of southern black sharecroppers; in 1931, as many as 6 blacks died when a 500-man posse in Camp Hill, Alabama, hunted down members of a black farmers' union after they met in a local church.

The sudden upsurge in antiblack activity spurred Walter White into more furious action than ever. As "the dismal decade of the thirties grew more and more dismal," he recalled later, "I found myself with less and less time for . . . the diversions which had formerly lightened the load of problems and hard work." Believing that antilynching legislation could succeed only with presidential support, White repeatedly urged Roosevelt to speak out against lynching. His nonstop appeals to the White House—which accounted for Eleanor Roosevelt's labeling him a "nuisance"—achieved little at first.

In 1933, however, the lynching toll reached 28: 24 blacks and 4 whites, 2 of them killed by a mob in San Jose, California. After the West Coast deaths, Roosevelt finally heeded White's advice and publicly condemned "that vile form of murder, lynch law, which has broken out in our midst anew." Addressing the nation on radio, the president said, "We know that it is murder, and a deliberate and definite disobedience of the commandment 'Thou shalt not kill.' We do not excuse those in high places or low who condone lynch law."

Roosevelt's words emboldened many who had opposed lynching but feared speaking out against the barbaric practice. After the presidential statement, said White, "we found support for [antilynching]

The body of Ab Young, a young black man falsely accused of shooting a white highway worker in 1935, hangs from a tree in Slayden, Mississippi. Young had been lynched by a mob of 50 white men, an act that the local prosecutor promised to "investigate thoroughly." No arrests were made in the case.

legislation from some who would have been most unlikely to give support even a few years before."

The new attitudes promised hope for the Costigan-Wagner Anti-Lynching Bill, a federal measure backed by White and the NAACP. Southern senators had blocked the bill in 1934 despite its endorsement by 10 state legislatures and more than 50 million private citizens. But by the following year, what White called "a tremendous volume of public opinion" in the bill's favor convinced him its time had come at last. All he needed was Roosevelt's solid backing.

White tried to make an appointment with the president. Time after time, however, White House aides intercepted the NAACP leader's letters and telegrams, showing none of them to the chief executive. At last, recalled White, "I turned in desperation to Mrs. Roosevelt."

A tall, intense woman with a deep sensitivity to human rights, Eleanor Roosevelt demonstrated a devotion to public service matched by few first ladies before or since. "Her enemies and critics used every device of criticism and slander to stop her," White wrote later, "but, undaunted, she continued to speak and act as her conscience dictated. She gave to many Americans, particularly Negroes, hope and faith which enabled them to continue the struggle for full citizenship." Walter White and Eleanor Roosevelt became close friends as well as allies in the fight for civil rights.

White's call to the first lady accomplished its goal; she promptly arranged for his interview with the president. Joining Roosevelt on the White House porch one spring Sunday in 1935, the NAACP leader stressed the urgent need for the president's support. Roosevelt listened with sympathy, but his political realism ruled the day. To bring the nation out of the depression, he needed new laws; to get those laws enacted, he needed the support of the Senate's powerful southern faction.

"I've got to get legislation passed by Congress to save America," he told White. "If I come out for the anti-lynching bill now, [the southern senators] will block every bill I ask Congress to pass to keep America from collapsing. I just can't take that risk."

In the end, southern senators defeated the Costigan-Wagner bill: In a typical attack on it, Senator "Cotton Ed" Smith of South Carolina called lynching "necessary" to "protect the fair womanhood of the South from beasts." Reintroduced in 1937 and 1938, the bill again failed to pass.

As it turned out, Congress never made lynching a federal crime. Thanks to White's relentless, decades-long campaign against it, however, Americans finally woke up to its evils. With the spotlight on lynching, the grim practice slowly diminished; by the mid-1960s, it would be virtually ended. "The most effective weapon against the crime," White would write in 1954, "has been the education of public opinion to the barbarity [and] the frequently obvious falsity of the excuses, such as rape, given by the lynchers."

Characteristically ignoring his own pivotal role, White said, "Many investigations of lynchings and race riots, sometimes made at the risk of injury or death to the investigators, have been made. The true facts thus uncovered have been publicized by the press . . . and on the floor of Congress. Carefully documented studies have exploded the falsehood that lynching is necessary for the protection of white women in the South." Most important, added White, had been the "moral conscience of the nation," which, once aroused, had "organized to force a change."

White may have downplayed his part in the fight for racial justice, but his colleagues did not. In 1937,

Gladys and Walter White relax at home before the 1937 ceremony at which he received the coveted Spingarn Medal. During the presentation, White's family listened proudly as future Supreme Court justice Frank Murphy made a speech that concluded, "and above all else, Walter is a true Christian gentleman." Murphy's words of praise, joked the former mischief maker from Atlanta, "almost made mother faint with astonishment."

Singer Marian Anderson gives a historic concert at the Lincoln Memorial, a site chosen by White. He picked the public monument for Anderson's 1939 Easter recital in Washington, D.C., after the Daughters of the American Revolution, an all-white social group that owned Constitution Hall, declared their magnificent auditorium off-limits to blacks.

the NAACP honored his heroic efforts to eradicate lynching by awarding him its coveted Spingarn Medal. The prize, its recipient decided by an independent award committee, had been initiated in 1914 by Joel E. Spingarn, then treasurer and later president of the NAACP. The medal is given annually for "the highest or noblest achievement by an American Negro."

Proudly receiving the 23rd annual medal, White joined illustrious company: Previous winners included writer, educator, and editor W. E. B. Du Bois, scientist George Washington Carver, educator Mary McLeod Bethune, and White's colleague and friend James Weldon Johnson.

The Spingarn award committee declined to name a medalist for 1938, but the following year, it found a worthy recipient: Marian Anderson, the great contralto who had been called "the voice of the

American soul." Fighting poverty and racial prejudice with calm courage, Anderson had broken the color line in classical music and become an internationally acclaimed star: "Yours is a voice," celebrated conductor Arturo Toscanini told the brilliant young singer, "one hears once in a hundred years." Another admirer, Walter White, said Anderson was incapable of singing "other than perfectly."

Soon after the Spingarn committee announced its selection of Anderson for the 1939 medal, the singer's manager, Sol Hurok, decided she should give a major concert in Washington, D.C. He selected Constitution Hall, the city's largest auditorium, as the concert site. Hurok asked the hall's owners, a group called the Daughters of the American Revolution (DAR), to reserve Sunday, April 9, for the performance. The DAR's response: Constitution Hall was unavailable to Miss Anderson on April 9 or any other date.

The DAR, an association of women whose ancestors had served in the American Revolution, accepted only whites as members—and, Hurok discovered, only white performers in its magnificent hall. Leaked to the press, the news of this blatant prejudice sent reporters straight to Walter White. Would he make a statement about the DAR? Realizing that "no one would be surprised to learn that [he] was indignant," White withheld comment. Instead of talking, he wired a host of well-known people and asked for their comments. Replies poured in almost at once.

Artists, singers, society figures, and politicians roared their indignation. "I am ashamed to play at Constitution Hall," said renowned violinist Jascha Heifetz. "No hall is too good for Marian Anderson," telegraphed New York mayor Fiorello La Guardia.

Next, White got a call from Eleanor Roosevelt, herself a member of the DAR. She planned to resign in protest, said the first lady, but she wanted White's opinion first. With his blessing, she quit the organization, an act that focused worldwide attention on the issue.

Another way to draw attention to the DAR's bigotry, and to prejudice in general, White decided, would be to present Anderson in a free, open-air concert in the nation's capital. He suggested the Lincoln Memorial as the ideal site. When Anderson and Hurok agreed, White asked Eleanor Roosevelt to recruit a sponsoring committee of cabinet members, Supreme Court justices, and other distinguished Washingtonians. Working with Roosevelt and Secretary of the Interior Harold Ickes—a man known for his sensitivity to racial injustice—White scheduled the concert for April 9, Easter Sunday.

As White drove his family to the Lincoln Memorial that afternoon, he worried that the weather might affect the turnout. Washington had been covered in a thin layer of snow the day before, and although the sun had reemerged, it was cold enough to keep the fainthearted indoors. But as White approached the memorial, his worry turned to delight. Facing the statue of the man who had freed the nation's slaves 76 years earlier, 75,000 people of all races stood together, ready to honor a great black artist.

From the opening bars of "America" to the last notes of the spiritual, "Nobody Knows the Trouble I've Seen," Anderson held the audience spellbound. When she finished, the crowd stood in absolute silence for a moment, then rushed toward her. White leapt to the microphone, urging calm. As he looked out on the sea of humanity, his gaze fell on a young black woman. Brightly dressed in Easter finery, she was stretching her arms toward Anderson.

White recalled that the young woman's hands, "despite their youth, had known only the dreary work of manual labor." Her face streamed with tears, but in her eyes, said White, "flamed hope bordering on ecstasy. . . . If Marian Anderson could do it, the girl's eyes seemed to say, then I can, too."

Not long after Anderson's triumphant concert, White received sad tidings: His mother had died at her home in Atlanta. Never admitting to more than 70, Madeline White was approaching her 80th birthday when her strong heart failed her at last. White grieved, but he felt none of the bitterness that had lashed him when his father died in misery in the dank "colored ward" of a city hospital.

"With the strong determination which had carried her through life," White recalled, his mother had turned down all her children's offers to come and live with them. "All you children were born here," she said firmly, "and I am going to stay right here until they carry me out." Madeline White had kept her house as spotless as ever, scrubbing, polishing, and repairing. Not long before her death, her son George had come home unexpectedly and found her, Walter White said, "perched precariously at the top of a swaying and shaky ladder, touching up with a paintbrush some spots under the eaves of the second story of the house."

Madeline White, as she had wished, ended her days in her own home, surrounded by family members and at peace with the world. "She died as she had lived—with courage," said her son Walter.

During the next few years, White was to need a large dose of that family courage himself.

8

BATTLEFRONTS

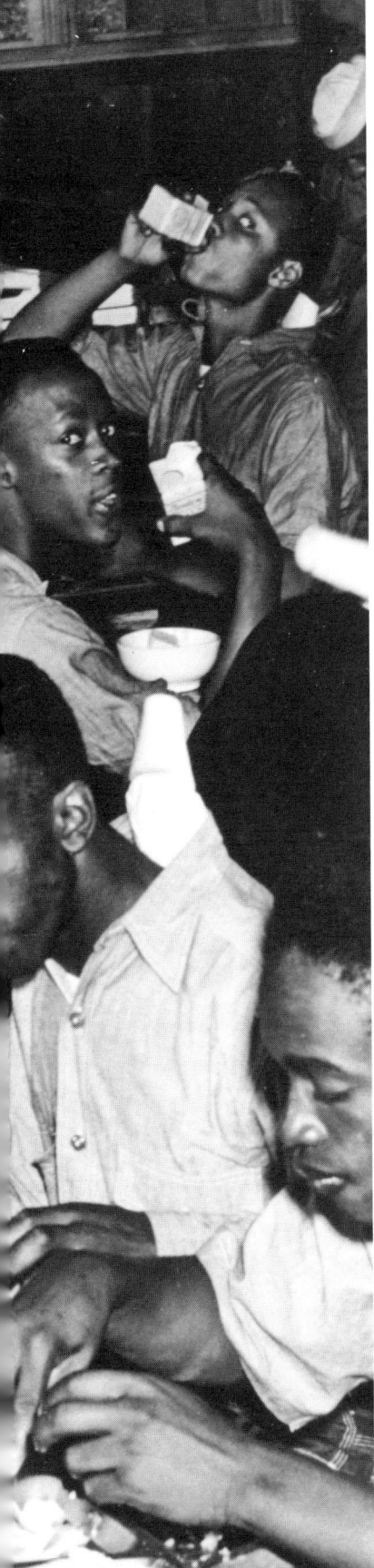

IN 1939, GERMANY'S Nazi forces invaded and conquered Poland. England and France responded by declaring war on Germany and its ally, Italy. World War II had begun. Meanwhile, Japan, which had been at war with China since 1937, continued its military expansion across the Pacific. In 1940, Germany conquered most of western Europe, including France, and Japan joined the German-Italian alliance. By this time, most Americans saw war as inevitable for their own nation.

To prepare for it, President Roosevelt began to enlarge the U.S. armed forces, expand America's arsenal, and supply military equipment to embattled Britain. War-goods factories sprang up across the nation, providing employment for millions of Americans and almost instantly ending the depression that had plagued the country for almost a decade. Left out of the prosperity, however, were blacks; most defense plants hired only white workers.

The armed forces offered blacks even less: "Jim Crow," observes historian William Manchester, "was practically a member of the military establishment." In 1940, the army's officer corps included two blacks;

Members of a black U.S. Army regiment share a meal during World War II. Until three years after the war's end, American troops ate, slept, worked, and fought in strictly segregated units. "Jim Crow," noted one historian, "was practically a member of the military establishment."

81

Labor leader and civil rights activist A. Philip Randolph founded the nation's first effective national black union, the Brotherhood of Sleeping Car Porters, in 1925. Joining forces with White in 1941, Randolph helped plan a giant protest march on Washington, aimed at persuading President Franklin Roosevelt to desegregate the armed forces and the defense industry.

the navy had no black officers at all. The three army regiments that accepted black recruits usually assigned them to such work as loading and unloading ships and trucks. Blacks who enlisted in the navy were almost always stationed in mess halls, where they wore short white jackets and served food to white officers.

Walter White aimed to change this situation. Joining forces with black labor leader A. Philip Randolph and National Urban League executive T. Arnold Hill, he requested a meeting with Roosevelt in September 1940. The three men asked the president to end racial discrimination in the defense industry and the armed forces.

Roosevelt, recalled White, "listened attentively and apparently sympathetically," but in the end, he did little. A month after the meeting, the White House announced a new policy on blacks in the armed forces: They would now be trained as pilots, aviation mechanics, and technical specialists, but military segregation would continue unchanged. The mingling of races in the services, said the president, "would produce situations destructive to morale and detrimental to the preparation for national defense." All current *and future* black army units would be commanded by white officers.

"Far from diminishing jimcrowism," reported a stunned White, "the new plan actually extended it!" On the subject of blacks in the defense industry, the government announcement said nothing.

White, Randolph, and Hill immediately issued a declaration of their own. "We are inexpressibly shocked," it said, "that a president of the United States at a time of national peril should [advocate] segregation. Official approval by the Commander-in-Chief of the Army and Navy [the president] of such discrimination . . . is a stab in the back of democracy."

In the uproar that followed this announcement, the government made a few minor concessions. William H. Hastie, the nation's first black federal judge, was appointed civilian aide to the secretary of war; Colonel Benjamin O. Davis, Sr., one of the army's two black officers, was promoted to brigadier general; Colonel Campbell Johnson, the army's other black officer, was named assistant to the director of the Selective Service (the national draft system). These men, said White, "worked valiantly," but they could accomplish only modest results in the face of ongoing official segregation.

As the Nazi armies continued to ravage Europe, England shuddered under relentless German attacks and America's entry into the war loomed ever closer. Defense factories began working around the clock, calling for more and more workers to help produce the machine guns, bombers, and tanks that now rolled from their great assembly lines. "But still," White noted, "the doors of war plants, with but few exceptions, remained closed to Negroes. Bitterness grew at an alarming pace throughout the country."

In the spring of 1941, A. Philip Randolph proposed a black protest march on Washington, to take place on July 4. Believing that it might improve the black labor situation, White threw the strength of the NAACP behind the march. The plan sent a tremor through official Washington.

On June 18, Roosevelt sent for White and Randolph, who once again stated their case for integration in the military and in defense. Once again, the president listened carefully, but he was clearly more worried about the proposed march and the damage it could do to the illusion of national unity. Getting to the real point of the meeting, he turned to White and said, "Walter, how many people will *really* march?"

"No less than one hundred thousand," White responded. "The president looked me full in the eye for a long time," he recalled. "Eventually he appeared to believe that I meant what I said."

"What do you want me to do?" the president asked the NAACP chief.

Patiently repeating their demands, White and Randolph said they wanted "the speediest possible abolition of discrimination in war industries and in the armed services."

On June 25, one week after the meeting—and nine days before the scheduled march—Roosevelt issued Executive Order 8802. Although it failed to address military integration, the directive established a Fair Employment Practices Committee (FEPC). This agency was designed to ensure equal access to jobs in the defense industries, "without discrimination because of race, creed, color, or country of national origin." White and Randolph called off the march.

Discontinued in 1944, the FEPC lacked real policing power, and it never received adequate funding to accomplish its mission fully. Nevertheless, its creation marked a turning point in the nation's social progress. "The great movement which eventually emerged from it," historian Manchester has observed, "would challenge all subsequent American presidents." According to White, "more progress was made by the FEPC toward employment on the basis of ability in the face of racial and religious discrimination than at any other period in American history."

After Japan bombed the U.S. naval base at Pearl Harbor, Hawaii, on December 7, 1941, the United States declared war against both Japan and Germany. Now the American war effort reached a crescendo; guns, tanks, bombs, ammunition, aircraft, and ships were needed in immense quantities and in record

Black volunteers sign up with a U.S. Army Air Corps recruiting officer in 1941, the first year in which the air force opened its ranks to nonwhites. But this slight improvement in military policy, obtained by the tireless efforts of White and other civil rights leaders, failed to end segregation in the armed forces; racial integration, said the nation's president, would be "destructive" to morale and to defense preparations.

time. That need, together with the FEPC, finally opened the doors of many defense factories to black workers.

"Numerous industrial plants," noted White, "which had not employed Negroes . . . previously, found that they were capable of as skilled performance as any other group." Offered work in these plants, thousands of southern blacks moved into the industrialized cities of the North. Detroit, center of much of the nation's war production, attracted particularly large numbers of blacks. Finding themselves in a city already straining at the seams with its wartime population, these newcomers settled wherever they could—often in fantastically overcrowded, rat-infested tenements.

Despite the wartime emergency and the FEPC, long-established racial prejudices continued to simmer in Detoit and other cities. Blacks bitterly resented their wretched housing, lack of recreational facilities, and the frequent insults they suffered from white workers. Whites regarded the blacks with fear, convinced that their own jobs would eventually be lost to these interlopers. In early June 1943, for example, the promotion of 3 black workers triggered a strike of 25,000 whites in a Detroit bomber-engine factory. "I'd rather see [Nazi leader Adolf] Hitler and [Japanese emperor] Hirohito win the war than work beside a nigger on the assembly line!" screamed one white striker.

White, who had been watching events in Detroit closely, expected an eruption of major violence. It came on Sunday, June 21. A fistfight between two men, one black, the other white, sent a series of wild rumors through the Michigan city: A white mob, said blacks, had hurled a black woman and her child into a lake; a mad black rapist was on the loose, said whites. In fact, no such events had occurred, but the stories swept through the city and set a nightmare into motion.

In the black ghetto, residents began stoning cars driven by whites, then destroying and looting white-owned shops and businesses. White mobs roamed the city, looking for blacks to beat. As soon as the mayhem began, the president of the NAACP's Detroit branch called White in New York. Within hours, he was on a plane, headed for the troubled midwestern city.

When he got there, the rioting was still in full swing, with blacks and whites assaulting one another on almost every street corner. People of both races set fires, smashed cars, broke into stores, and seized arms from pawnshops and sporting goods shops. Gunfire filled the air.

The city's white majority, however, soon got the upper hand, dragging blacks out of movie theaters, automobiles, and streetcars, and beating, stabbing, or shooting them. Meanwhile, observed a horrified White, the city's largely white police force "stood by and made no effort to check the assaults." Worse, many policemen joined the attacks themselves.

White saw one white officer diverting cars driven by blacks into a street where an armed white mob

Detroit whites drag a black victim out of a streetcar during the 1943 riot. When city and state officials ignored White's pleas for action, the NAACP chief personally appealed to the U.S. War Department, which sent federal troops to restore order.

awaited them. In another part of town, a police captain boarded a streetcar, announced that a white mob was lying in wait, and offered to escort the car's eight black passengers to safety. "Four of the Negroes accepted the offer," White recounted, "and were promptly turned over to the mob to be beaten to death."

Despite White's pleas, neither Detroit's mayor nor his police commissioner made any move to halt the violence. White then called on Michigan's governor, Harry S. Kelly, and begged him to send for federal troops to check the mobs. Kelly also proved ineffectual. In desperation, White telephoned the War Department itself. "Federal troops reached the city at nightfall," he reported, "a curfew was established, and order was restored."

Joining their boss after the Detroit riot are NAACP assistant executive secretary Roy Wilkins (left) and NAACP Legal Defense Fund chief Thurgood Marshall (right). Although they produced hefty evidence and numerous eyewitnesses, the NAACP executives had no success in obtaining convictions—or even reprimands—for the Detroit policemen who had beaten and killed blacks during the bloody upheaval.

Detroit's 30 hours of rioting resulted in the death of 34 people, 9 of them white and 25 black. Of the 600 seriously injured Detroiters, 75 percent were black, as were 85 percent of the 1,832 people arrested. But in the midst of this senseless death and destruction, White did find something positive: There were, he said, "many instances of Negroes defending their white neighbors and white neighbors protecting Negro friends."

Although White had been instrumental in ending Detroit's murderous spree, he was unable to obtain justice for its victims. Future Supreme Court justice Thurgood Marshall, then head of the NAACP's Legal Defense Fund, joined White in Detroit; the two men battled to get state authorities to take some action against city policemen who had attacked blacks during the rioting, but to no avail. "We were never able even to have them queried or reprimanded, much less punished," reported the frustrated White.

But one politician—New York City's mayor, Fiorello H. La Guardia—showed deep concern about the violence in Detroit, and about its chances of breaking out elsewhere. When White returned to Manhattan, La Guardia asked him to help design a plan to deal with rioting if it occurred in New York. Neither White nor the mayor expected immediate trouble, but it arrived about a month later.

The 1943 Harlem riot was triggered less by racial tension than by a backlog of long-stifled anger and frustration. For white Americans, the Great Depression was fast fading into history, but most black Americans still found it almost impossible to provide adequate food, clothing, and housing for their families.

Billboards, newspapers, and radios trumpeted patriotic wartime messages, reminding the nation that it enjoyed not only freedom but the world's highest standard of living. To blacks, such messages contained bitter irony. Aggravating their enduring poverty were frequent reports of the mistreatment of black soldiers overseas. Sons, sweethearts, brothers, and fathers were risking their life for their country, yet their country continued to treat them as second-class citizens.

On the sweltering Sunday afternoon of August 1, 1943, a white policeman in Harlem tried to arrest a black woman on a charge of public drunkenness. The woman protested, and a black soldier, home on leave, went to her aid. In the ensuing scuffle, the police officer suffered a cracked head, and the soldier a bullet wound in the shoulder. As in Detroit, the incident quickly inspired ugly rumors.

Throughout Harlem, residents told each other that the policeman had murdered the soldier in cold blood. This false news brought the tensions in Harlem to a head. In a 24-hour period of rioting, angry blacks surged through the streets, assailing whites and destroying hundreds of white-owned stores and other businesses.

That evening, bone tired from his Detroit investigation and a nonstop series of lectures around the country, White went to bed early. He told his wife that he "did not want to be disturbed under any circumstances, even if President Roosevelt or Cleopatra called." Moments later, the phone rang: "There is a riot going on in Harlem," said an NAACP staff member. Next came a call from La Guardia himself, asking White to meet him at once at Harlem's central police station. White grabbed a cab and headed for 125th Street.

By the time White joined La Guardia at the Harlem station house, the mayor had already called in both police reinforcements and military policemen (MPs) from the local army base. Noting that all the MPs were white, the NAACP chief suggested that

White (center, hands on hips) watches New York City policemen assemble outside Harlem's central police station on August 2, 1943. The night before, the NAACP chief had helped calm a Harlem riot triggered by false reports of white police brutality.

the mayor call for an equal number of black soldiers. The furious crowds believed that a white officer had killed a black soldier, and White knew the MPs would be safer in racially mixed pairs.

White and other peacemakers spent the rest of the night riding through Harlem in city-owned sound trucks, broadcasting the same message over and over: The black soldier was only slightly wounded and in no danger. "Go to your homes!" White shouted. "Don't destroy in one night the reputations as good citizens you have taken a lifetime to build! Go home—now!"

At first, the mob pelted White's truck with bricks and bottles, but gradually his words sank in. By dawn, he said, "the fury of the mob had spent itself," and quiet descended over the shattered streets of Harlem. The riot's final toll: 6 dead, 543 injured. Grim enough, the figures would probably have been even higher without La Guardia and White's quick thinking and courage.

White knew the Harlem riot had stemmed from a number of roots: economic oppression, wretched housing, inadequate job opportunities, and segregated and inferior public facilities. Perhaps highest on the list of black grievances in 1943, however, was the hostility shown to America's black servicemen—not by the enemy, but by their fellow citizens.

"A steady stream of letters had poured [into Harlem] from Camp Stewart, Georgia, written by men of the 369th Infantry and telling of gratuitous insults and beatings and humiliations suffered by men who had fought in the Pacific and had been returned home to train other fighters," he noted. "Not only Harlem's newspapers but the daily press had been filled with countless stories of lynchings and mistreatment of Negro soldiers."

Treatment of black soldiers was said to be even worse overseas than on the home front. White decided that something had to be done—and that he was the man to do it. Accredited as a war correspondent, he took off for Europe on January 2, 1944.

9

"I'VE GOT WORK TO DO"

WHITE'S WARTIME TRAVELS took him across Europe, into the Middle East and North Africa, and onto the islands of the Pacific. He carried the credentials of a correspondent—and actually sent many dispatches to the *New York Post*—but news reporting was not his main mission. The 50-year-old crusader was flying thousands of miles, often over enemy territory, entering battle zones, and living with his nation's servicemen for one main reason: "To learn first hand the facts about the clashes between white and Negro American soldiers which seeped through to us despite wartime censorship." White (who would chronicle his mission in a 1945 book, *A Rising Wind: A Report of the Negro Soldier in the European Theater of War*) was to discover that the reality was even worse than the rumors.

In all the theaters of war, White saw combat-trained black recruits relegated to service units; these men cooked and served food, built roads, drove supply trucks, and unloaded ships. Assigned to segregated quarters, black troops were also restricted to their own mess halls, theaters, service clubs, and transportation. Morale among black soldiers was understandably low.

White went from base to base, talking to officers and enlisted men of all races and putting together a file of cases. "I came across innumerable instances

Suited up as an official war correspondent, White prepares to leave for the European front in early 1944. Although he filed frequent news reports from overseas, the NAACP leader's primary mission was to investigate America's treatment of its black troops.

where Negro soldiers were court-martialed, found guilty, and sentenced to long terms for minor offenses," he wrote. Meanwhile, he added, "white soldiers who were guilty of much graver crimes were either acquitted or meted out light punishment."

Nevertheless, said White, most of America's fighting men "were either decent in their racial attitudes or indifferent on the subject." He found that many prejudiced white soldiers lost their racial animosities when they actually fought alongside blacks. "One of the most dramatic examples of the abandonment of interracial antagonisms in combat," he noted, "occurred during and after the Battle of the Bulge."

Fought in Belgium in late 1944, this crucial battle began with a massive surprise German counteroffensive against the American army. Frantically trying to halt the German advance, U.S. commanders used every available soldier, but they desperately needed more. Finally, the military appealed to black Service of Supply soldiers to volunteer for combat duty. "An avalanche of volunteers" responded, reported White. "We've been giving a lot of sweat," one black recruit told White. "Now I think we'll mix some blood with it!"

Also shifted—at their own request—to direct combat were the men of the all-black 969th Field Artillery Battalion. The black troops fought the Battle of the Bulge with extraordinary valor. After the five-week encounter, several men of the 969th received the Distinguished Service Cross, the Silver Star, and other citations for courage. General Maxwell D. Taylor, commander of the all-white 101st Airborne Division, later wrote to the 969th's commanding officer: "This division," he said, "is proud to have shared the battlefield with your command."

White reported that after the great battle—a resounding victory for U.S. forces—the army took a poll of white officers and enlisted men, asking their feelings about serving with black troops. He was surprised and heartened by the poll's findings: Before the battle, 77 percent of the men had opposed integration; after it, 77 percent favored it. Typical of the remarks made to White were those of an Alabama sergeant who admitted that at first, he had bitterly resented serving with black troops. "I used to think they would be yellow in combat," he said, "but I seen them work."

Black troops continued to serve with gallantry and distinction throughout World War II. The all-black 332nd Fighter Group, for example, flew 1,579 missions, destroyed 260 enemy planes, damaged 148 others, and sank a German destroyer. Ninety-five of the 332nd's pilots received the Distinguished Flying Cross, and 744 won Air Medals and Clusters.

The first black armored unit to see combat was the 761st Tank Battalion. Sending them into battle, legendary general George S. Patton had said: "Men, you're the first Negro tankers ever to fight in the American Army. I would never have asked for you if you weren't good. I don't care what color you are so long as you go up there and kill those Kraut SOBs." Commended for showing "conspicuous courage," the 761st spent 183 days in action; 10 of its tanks were chosen to be in the honor guard when the Germans surrendered in Reims, France, on May 7, 1945.

Before he left Europe, White called on General Dwight Eisenhower, commander in chief of Allied forces in Western Europe, and summarized the problems faced by black troops. The general, who "seemed gravely disturbed" by White's reports, asked him to make a list of "recommendations for whatever action could be undertaken to correct or ease the situation." White promptly provided such a list of actions.

Urgently needed, he said, was the establishment

Colonel Benjamin O. Davis, Jr., prepares to board his P-47 Thunderbolt in 1944. Son of the U.S. Army's first black general, Davis commanded the all-black 332nd Fighter Group, one of the most highly decorated aircraft fighter units of World War II.

Members of a mortar company of the all-black 92nd Infantry Division pound the enemy during World War II. Known as the Buffalo Division because of its service in the post–Civil War American West, the 92nd lost 3,000 men during the bloody 1944 invasion of Italy; collectively, the division won 65 Silver Stars, 162 Bronze Stars, and 1,300 Purple Hearts.

of a biracial board to review court-martial records of black troops. He also urged the abolition of the numerous areas declared off-limits to black soldiers, the assignment of racially mixed military police teams, the use of black air units on a desegregated basis, the assignment of black doctors to the Medical Corps, and an end to the practice of using black combat troops in service units.

Eisenhower, who had often praised his army's black members, issued stern orders against racial discrimination and assigned a team to study White's demands. Nevertheless, he continued to insist, even after the war, on the necessity for racial segregation in the army.

By the time Germany surrendered, White was thousands of miles from Europe, looking into the situation of the nation's black troops in the Pacific theater. Flying from one battle-scarred island to another—Hawaii, Guam, Leyte, Luzon, Dutch New Guinea—he found things much as they were in Europe: Although most black soldiers fought bravely, they continued to receive abuse, and often injustice, from white officers and fellow enlisted men.

At the end of his Pacific tour, White met with General Douglas MacArthur, Allied supreme commander of the Southwest Pacific. As he had with Eisenhower, White presented a documented list of cases, incidents, and practices that resulted in racial injustice in the military. As Eisenhower had done, MacArthur questioned White closely, then said he would look into the charges. Little changed.

World War II ended with Allied victory in August 1945. At this point, the army ordered most of the black platoons out of the combat divisions, reassigning them to menial jobs in service units. "It was apparent," said White, "that powerful forces in the Army were determined that, however well Negroes had fought and behaved, they should not have the glory and publicity of returning to America as part of the victorious combat divisions or be permitted to wear the insignia of those divisions."

White's constant jabbing at the white military conscience, however, had not been in vain. In 1948, three years after the war's end, the United States would desegregate its armed forces at last. White, of course, had not been alone in working toward this goal: Other voices of reform, notably those of the black press and labor leader A. Philip Randolph, had also maintained ongoing attacks on military segregation. But White's steady drumbeat of demands had perhaps sounded the strongest note in the thunderous chorus of protest.

After he returned from the Pacific in 1945, White was named a consultant to the American delegation at the founding meeting of the United Nations. Appalled to discover that his country had no intention of supporting a proposed human rights declaration in the UN charter, White spoke out, insisting that America "use the moral leadership which its resources and geographic position gave it as to no other nation."

As he and several like-minded observers publicized their views, White recalled, "an alarmed and highly vocal public opinion began to make itself felt." The American delegation slowly edged toward a stronger position on world human rights, helping, said White, "to make the flowery phrases of freedom more nearly a reality."

But at home, violent racism once again stalked the land. Black servicemen had served their country with dedication and courage, but after the war, many whites were determined that these veterans remember "their place." During what White called the "terrible summer of 1946," five blacks, two of them veterans and two of them women, were lynched in Georgia and Louisiana. In South Carolina, a small-

Admiral Chester Nimitz, commander in chief of the U.S. Pacific fleet, awards the Navy Cross to messman Dorie Miller, one of the first American heroes of World War II. Serving on the USS Arizona *during the 1941 Japanese attack on Pearl Harbor, Hawaii, Miller had seized a fallen shipmate's antiaircraft gun and, in a burst of inspired marksmanship, shot down six Japanese planes. But the navy never promoted Miller; still a messman, he was killed in action two years after Pearl Harbor.*

White confers with the family of a man lynched during the wave of Klan-inspired violence that followed World War II. When the NAACP leader described the escalating mob murders to Democratic president Harry S. Truman, the shocked chief executive promised to take action; true to his word, he immediately ordered a sweeping investigation of civil rights violations and, in 1948, desegregated the U.S. armed forces and all federal agencies.

town police chief beat and permanently blinded a black veteran after a minor dispute on a bus.

Hoping to spur presidential action against the new wave of terror, White called on President Harry S. Truman in September. The president, who had taken office after Roosevelt's death in April 1945, listened in increasing horror as White detailed the recent lynchings and the blinding of the veteran. "My God!" he said. "I had no idea it was as terrible as that! We've got to do something!"

What the president did, with White's approval, was to set up the Committee on Civil Rights, a group empowered to investigate civil liberties violations and recommend a program to correct them. Believing that such "especially interested" people as himself might diminish the impact of the committee, White chose not to join it. Instead, he suggested a panel that included major figures in industry, labor, law, education, and religion.

The committee's report, entitled *To Secure These Rights*, was, said White, "without doubt the most courageous and specific document of its kind in American history." Beneath it, he added, was "the ominous rumble of a warning that if these rights are not secured to all Americans, there soon will be no rights for any." Unflinchingly detailing the grim prospects faced by the nation's blacks in housing, jobs, and law, the document called for sweeping reforms, including the passage of 27 civil rights acts.

True to his promise to White, Truman gave Congress a massive program of civil rights legislation; southern senators, however, defeated each of the measures in early 1948. Truman refused to give in: In July 1948, he issued two historic executive orders, one desegregating the armed forces, the other ordering all federal agencies to practice scrupulous fair employment policies.

White must have felt a surge of satisfaction about Truman's bold moves, both of them actions the

NAACP chief had championed for decades. Satisfying as his work was, however, it took a heavy personal toll. He had suffered a heart attack in 1947, bringing a stern warning from his doctors: Slow down or prepare to die. In the same year, White's 24-year marriage, long strained by his frequent absences and nonstop work habits, quietly came to an end. Proud parents of two grown, college-educated children, Gladys and Walter White remained good friends after their 1947 divorce.

White had proved himself a master of many arts, but slowing down was not among them. He continued to run the NAACP, give lectures, act as a UN adviser, organize rallies, attend national and international conferences, and write—magazine articles, a new book, and a twice-weekly newspaper column.

White, who had been planning to write his memoirs for some years, finally got down to work on *A Man Called White* in 1948. An old friend, Poppy Cannon, volunteered to help him organize his records and type the manuscript. A prominent advertising executive, the author of several cookbooks and business manuals, and the divorced mother of three children, Cannon had first met White in 1929. The two, who had taken an immediate liking to one another, had often met over the years; Cannon, in fact, was one of the first people White sought out after his father's tragic death.

As White struggled with his mountains of notes and Cannon offered discreet editorial advice, the couple's relationship deepened. Finally, they decided to marry, although they knew the move would generate widespread controversy: Born in South Africa, Cannon was white.

Interracial marriage was not only a shocking notion to many Americans of the era; it was actually illegal in several states. But White had spent most of his life preaching racial equality, and the prospect of a public uproar left him unshaken. Of course, the two could have avoided friction by remaining unmarried, but White refused to consider such a solution: "In my family," he said firmly, "we marry the women we love."

What did worry White was the possibility that his marriage might harm the NAACP. To forestall trouble, he offered his resignation to the organization's board of directors. Its members immediately rejected it, giving White a year's leave of absence instead.

After a quiet wedding at Cannon's Connecticut home in 1949, the couple departed on their honeymoon, a trip that White characteristically combined with business. Among his many affiliations was the Round the World Town Meeting, a program that sent Americans overseas to hold informal, open discussions with other nations' political and cultural leaders.

White and Cannon, who shared her husband's passionate concern for human rights, visited Europe, North Africa, the Middle East, and Asia. Wherever they went, the conversation inevitably turned to the current state of civil rights in America. Guardedly optimistic, White told his hosts that the crusade for racial justice had begun to achieve results but that it was still far from success.

When the Whites returned to America, they found—to their pleasant surprise—that most newspapers, even in the South, had reported their marriage as straight news. The public, too, proved quite accepting, a sure sign that times were changing. The loudest criticism of White's interracial marriage came from the black press—and from the NAACP itself.

From the time he became the NAACP's chief executive, White had held almost total control of the NAACP and its policies, a situation resented by a number of people within the organization. The

Gathered in New Delhi, members of the Round the World Town Meeting confer with Indian prime minister Jawaharlal Nehru (right) in August 1949. To Nehru's right are White and his new wife, Poppy Cannon, a South African writer whose dedication to racial justice matched his own.

controversy surrounding White's marriage seemed to provide an opportunity to wrestle some, if not all, of his power away. When White heard the low rumblings of discontent, he immediately withdrew his offer of resignation. Walking away from a fight was not his style.

The next NAACP election meeting turned out to be one of the bitterest in the organization's 40-year history. For hours, White's opponents campaigned for his ouster while his equally vehement supporters defended him and his record of undisputed achievement. Eleanor Roosevelt was among the many NAACP members who spoke on her friend's behalf. "The association," she said, needs his *leadership*, breadth and vision."

The NAACP finally voted to retain White as secretary, but to divide his once supreme authority among four executives. The decision, which left White no choice but to slow down, probably prolonged his life: His health was steadily declining. His services, however, were in as much demand as ever.

The White House offered him the governorship of the Virgin Islands; he turned it down. "Nobody's going to shut me up in a tropical paradise," he told his wife. "I've got work to do."

Next, Truman tried to persuade him to become ambassador to either Haiti or India. Again White refused: "Me carry out the dictates of the State Department?" he snorted. "They'd fire me so fast, but maybe not quite as fast as I'd fire myself." White's prominence also brought lucrative offers from the business community, but wealth had never been among his objectives. He had lived comfortably on his modest NAACP salary, and he had no wish to exploit his fame by leaving the NAACP for a cushy job in the private sector.

With more time available, White began to write *How Far the Promised Land?* (1955), a book in which he evaluated America's progress toward civil rights. For the most part ignoring his doctors' orders, he also kept his normal frantic schedule. White came to regard death as a "respected companion," said his friend and NAACP associate Clarence Mitchell. "There seemed to be an agreement between them," noted Mitchell, "that he would continue his busy life as though it was not necessary to prepare for the journey that this companion would one day insist that he must make."

Deeply concerned about her 61-year-old husband's casual attitude toward his health, Poppy Cannon approached the subject one day in 1955. She described the scene in her 1956 memoir, *A Gentle Knight: My Husband, Walter White*. "Have you ever thought that perhaps you might be more useful, and live longer outside the Association?" she asked. "I know that in the last few years you have become more and more interested in the world picture."

"Walter looked stricken," reported Cannon. " 'But the NAACP is my heart,' he said almost

Famed for his courageous NAACP leadership and tireless crusade for civil rights, White was also celebrated for his warmth, wit, and capacity for friendship. At his death in 1955, thousands of people expressed their love and respect: "Walter was a great man but he never ceased to be a 'nice guy,' " said a Manhattan executive. But a little girl from South Carolina may have put it even better: "He was a friend to the many American," she wrote. "He were not trying to live for him self alone, he was a man. Devoted to going up and not dropping down. He had a world wide love in his heart."

bashfully, like a young man confessing his secret love."

The next day, March 28, 1955, White was dead, felled by a final, massive heart attack.

Ten thousand people gathered for White's funeral. The grieving crowd included people of all races and economic classes, from ambassadors and senators to secretaries and elevator operators. "Not only the church but the streets, where there were loudspeakers, and the doorways and the windows for blocks around were thronged," White's widow wrote later. Another mourner recalled that "the church was too full. I was on the street—all of us silent, and a little child cried. From one of the windows a woman's voice said: 'Hold quiet, son, a great man has died.' "

Pouring in from all over the world, tributes to White emphasized the tremendous changes he had brought about. When he took over as NAACP secretary in 1931, the organization had shrunk to 70,000 members and an income of $59,000. At his death, its membership roll had grown to 250,000, its annual income to $500,000. During the two dozen years of his leadership, the NAACP helped move a reluctant nation, slowly, painfully, but steadily toward racial justice.

With White at its helm, the NAACP dealt a death blow to Jim Crow, eliminating barriers against black voters in the South, reversing unjust military convictions of black soldiers, and opening the doors to equal accommodation for all races in graduate schools, housing, public transportation, and recreational facilities.

And thanks to White and the incomparable Thurgood Marshall, whom White had appointed as head of the NAACP Legal Defense Fund in 1939, the U.S. Supreme Court finally outlawed public school segregation in a landmark 1954 decision, *Brown v. Board of Education.* "One devoted and tireless human being can work miracles, if he keeps forever at the cause," observed columnist Thomas Stokes. "[The] decision banning segregation in public schools was a memorial to Walter White."

Another of White's countless admirers, historian William Miles Brewer, called the NAACP chief "a foeman more than equal to the steel of any opponent." Brewer reminded Americans that White had "brazenly entered the communities of 41 lynchings and 8 race riots. . . . On more than one occasion, he escaped in the very nick of time similar fates of the lynched victims whose mutilations and executions he investigated. The sheer heroism of these adventures has few parallels in history."

White "lived, breathed and walked civil rights," said Congressman Adam Clayton Powell. "As long as history lasts, and there is the cry for full human freedom, Walter White's name will be echoed down the corridors of time. . . . He magnified civil rights to such a degree that the walls of prejudice, segregation, and discrimination came tumbling down."

In its obituary of White, the *New York Times* added another note: "Blue-eyed and fair of color, Walter White did not need to identify himself as a Negro. He did so deliberately, and in its way this act made a special mockery of race discrimination."

But perhaps White himself best summarized his attitude: "I am white and I am black," he said. "Black is white and white is black. When one shoots the other he kills his reflection. Only hate, the negative force, can separate them; only love, the positive force, can bind them together."

CHRONOLOGY

1893	Born Walter Francis White on July 1 in Atlanta, Georgia
1916	Graduates from Atlanta University
1918	Becomes assistant secretary of National Association for the Advancement of Colored People (NAACP); moves to New York City; undertakes first lynching investigation
1919	Investigates massacre of blacks in Phillips County, Arkansas
1922	Marries Leah Gladys Powell
1924	Publishes novel about bigotry, *The Fire in the Flint*
1926	Publishes second novel, *Flight*
1929	Publishes a study of lynching, *Rope and Faggot: A Biography of Judge Lynch*
1930	Successfully opposes confirmation of Supreme Court nominee Judge John J. Parker
1931	Becomes secretary (chief executive officer) of NAACP
1933	Establishes friendship with First Lady Eleanor Roosevelt
1937	Receives Spingarn Medal for efforts to eradicate lynching
1939	Organizes historic Marian Anderson concert in Washington, D.C.
1941	Persuades President Franklin D. Roosevelt to establish federal Fair Employment Practices Committee
1943	Instrumental in calming race riots in Detroit and New York City
1944	Visits World War II battlefronts to study mistreatment of black American servicemen
1945	Becomes adviser to the United Nations
1946	Meets with President Harry S. Truman; helps form Committee on Civil Rights
1947	Suffers first heart attack; divorces Gladys White
1948	Publishes autobiography, *A Man Called White*
1949	Marries Poppy Cannon
1955	Dies of a heart attack on March 28 at age 61; final book, *How Far the Promised Land?*, is published posthumously

FURTHER READING

Aptheker, Herbert, ed. *A Documentary History of the Negro People in the United States, 1910–1932.* Secaucus, NJ: Citadel Press, 1973.

Cannon, Poppy. *A Gentle Knight: My Husband, Walter White.* New York: Rinehart & Co., 1956.

Hoff-Wilson, Joan, and Marjorie Lightman, eds. *Without Precedent: The Life and Career of Eleanor Roosevelt.* Bloomington: Indiana Press, 1984.

Kirby, John B. *Black Americans in the Roosevelt Era.* Knoxville: University of Tennessee Press, 1980.

Manchester, William. *The Glory and the Dream: A Narrative History of America, 1932–1972.* Boston: Little, Brown, 1974.

Myrdal, Gunnar. *An American Dilemma.* New York: Harper & Brothers, 1944.

Rogers, Donald I. *Since You Went Away.* New Rochelle, NY: Arlington House, 1973.

Waldron, Edward E. *Walter White and the Harlem Renaissance.* Port Washington, NY: Kennikat Press, 1978.

White, Walter. *The Fire in the Flint.* New York: Knopf, 1924.

———. *Flight.* New York: Knopf, 1926.

———. *How Far the Promised Land?* New York: Viking Press, 1955.

———. *A Man Called White.* New York: Viking Press, 1948.

———. *A Rising Wind: A Report on the Negro Soldier in the European Theater of War.* New York: Doubleday, 1945.

———. *Rope and Faggot: A Biography of Judge Lynch.* New York: Knopf, 1929.

Woodward, C. Vann. *The Strange Career of Jim Crow.* 3rd ed. New York: Oxford University Press, 1974.

INDEX

Aiken, South Carolina, 52, 53, 55
American Language, The (Mencken), 49
Anderson, Marian, 76–77, 78, 79
Atlanta, Georgia, 19, 22, 23, 24, 25, 26, 31, 32, 47
Atlanta Journal, 24
Atlanta University, 20, 29
Autobiography of an Ex-Colored Man, The (Johnson), 49

Baltimore Evening Sun, 49
Battle of the Bulge, 94
Bethune, Mary McLeod, 76
Brewer, William Miles, 105
Brough, Charles H., 43
Brown v. Board of Education, 105

Camp Hill, Alabama, 72
Cannon, Poppy, 99, 100, 102, 104
Carver, George Washington, 76
Chicago, Illinois, 39, 40
Chicago Daily News, 44
Civil War, 13, 15
Clansman, The (Dixon), 24
Clarke, Edward Young, 46
Coatesville, Pennsylvania, 38
Committee on Civil Rights, 98
Constitution Hall, 77
Costigan-Wagner Anti-Lynching Bill, 74, 75
Crisis, The, 64–65
Cullen, Countee, 47
Curtis, Charles, 64

Daughters of the American Revolution (DAR), 77–78
Davis, Benjamin O., Sr., 83
Detroit, Michigan, 85, 86, 87, 88, 89
Dixon, Thomas, 24
Douglas, Aaron, 47
Du Bois, W. E. B., 35, 76

Eisenhower, Dwight, 95, 96
Estill Springs, Tennessee, 11, 12, 16, 17, 38
Executive Order 8802, 84

Fair Employment Practices Committee (FEPC), 84, 85
Fauset, Jessie, 47
Fire in the Flint, The, 50–52, 57, 58
Flight, 57–58
Fourteenth Amendment, 15

Gentle Knight: My Husband, Walter White (Cannon), 102
Great Depression, 60, 71, 88
Guggenheim Foundation, 58

Harlem, 88, 89, 90, 91
Harlem Renaissance, 47
Hastie, William H., 83
Heifetz, Jascha, 77
Hill, T. Arnold, 82
Hoover, Herbert, 60–61, 62
Howard, H. H., 52
How Far the Promised Land?, 102
Hughes, Langston, 47
Hurok, Sol, 77, 78
Hurston, Zora Neale, 47

Ickes, Harold, 78
Illinois Central Railroad, 72

Jim Crow laws, 14, 15, 81, 104

Johnson, Campbell, 83
Johnson, Hall, 47
Johnson, J. Henry, 55
Johnson, James Weldon, 34, 35, 37, 38, 41, 49–50, 59, 65, 76

Kelly, Harry S., 87
Key, James L., 31–32
Ku Klux Klan, 14, 24, 46, 51, 53, 54, 55

La Guardia, Fiorello, 77, 88, 89, 90
Legal Defense Fund, 88, 104
Lewis, Sinclair, 51, 57, 58
Lowman family, 52–53
Lynch, Charles, 59
Lynchings, 11, 12, 14, 15–16, 37, 38, 39, 53, 55, 59, 65, 66, 71, 72, 75, 91, 97, 98, 105

MacArthur, Douglas, 96
McIlherron, Jim, 11, 12, 16, 17, 38
McKay, Claude, 47
Main Street (Lewis), 51
Man Called White, A, 16, 99
Manchester, William, 81, 84
Marshall, Thurgood, 88, 104
Martin, Eugene, 68
Mencken, H. L., 49
Mitchell, Clarence, 102
Motley, Archibald, 47

Nash, Royal Freeman, 35
National Association for the Advancement of Colored People (NAACP)
  and antilynching legislation, 38, 74

Atlanta chapter, 32, 34
and Atlanta school board, 31
divides White's authority, 101
income, 104
membership, 37, 104
mission, 37
offers White a job, 34–35
and Phillips County Massacre, 44
protests Parker's nomination to Supreme Court, 62, 63, 64–65
sends White to Chicago riots, 40
and Spingarn Medal, 76, 77
and Supreme Court, 44–45
National Urban League, 82
New York City, 35, 37, 47
New York Post, 93
New York Times, 105
New York World, 51
969th Field Artillery Battalion, 94

Outlook, 72
Overman, Lee, 63

Parker, John J., 61–62, 63, 64, 65
Patton, George S., 95
Peonage, 41
Phillips County, Arkansas, 40, 41, 43, 45
Piedmont Hotel, 22
Plessy, Homer, 15
Plessy v. Ferguson, 15, 30
Poll taxes, 33–34
Powell, Adam Clayton, 105
Powell, Leah Gladys. *See* White, Gladys
Powell, Madrenne, 45
Progressive Farmers and Household Union of America, 42

Race riots
  Chicago, 39, 40
  Detroit, 86–88
  Harlem, 88, 89, 90

Randolph, A. Philip, 82, 83, 84, 97
Reconstruction, 13–14
Record, the Columbia, South Carolina, 55
Red Summer of 1919, 39
Rising Wind, A, 93
Roosevelt, Eleanor, 71, 72, 74, 77–78, 101
Roosevelt, Franklin Delano, 71, 72, 74–75, 81, 82, 83, 84, 98
Rope and Faggot: A Biography of Judge Lynch, 59
Round the World Town Meeting, 100

Savannah Press, 51
761st Tank Battalion, 95
Sharecropping, 41, 42, 72
Smart Set, The, 50
Smith, "Cotton Ed," 75
Spingarn, Joel E., 76
Spingarn Medal, 76–77
Standard Life Insurance Company, 29, 30, 35
Stokes, Thomas, 105
Storey, Moorfield, 44, 45
Supreme Court, U.S., 15, 30, 44, 45, 61, 62, 63, 104

Taylor, Maxwell D., 94
Thirteenth Amendment, 41
332nd Fighter Group, 95
Toomer, Jean, 47
Toscanini, Arturo, 77
To Secure These Rights, 98
Truman, Harry S., 98, 102

United Nations, 97

Waco, Texas, 38
Washingon, D.C., 66, 77
White, George (father), 19, 20–21, 22, 25, 26, 35, 68, 69

White, Gladys (wife), 45, 47, 49, 99
White, Jane (daughter), 58
White, Madeline (mother), 19, 21–22, 24, 79
White, Walter
  and antilynching legislation, 65, 66–67, 72, 74, 75
  arrival in New York, 37
  autobiography, 16–17, 23, 35, 40, 46, 53, 66, 99
  birth, 19
  death, 104
  divorce, 104
  education, 20, 21, 29
  fights armed forces segregation, 82–85, 91, 93–97
  in France, 58
  heart attacks, 99, 104
  investigates lynchings, 11–12, 16–17, 52–55
  and Ku Klux Klan, 46–47, 54, 55
  marriages, 45, 99–100, 101
  as novelist, 50–52, 57
  opposes Parker's nomination to Supreme Court, 61–65
  at Piedmont Hotel, 22–23
  and race riots, 39–43, 85–89, 105
  receives Spingarn Medal, 76
  religious training, 20
  replaces Johnson as NAACP chief, 65
  skin color, 22, 23, 26, 27, 40
  at Standard Life Insurance, 29, 30, 35
  and United Nations, 97, 99
  as war correspondent, 91, 93
  in Washington, D.C., 66
White, Walter, Jr. (son), 58
Wilson, Woodrow, 38
World War I, 39
World War II, 81, 84, 95, 96

PICTURE CREDITS

AP/Wide World Photos: pp. 3, 27, 33, 53, 70–71, 87, 90; Arkansas History Commission: pp. 43 (1595.2), 44 (1595.11); Atlanta Historical Society: pp. 18, 23, 24; The Bettmann Archive: pp. 80–81, 96; Collection of American Literature, Beinecke Library, Yale University: pp. 2–3, 28–29, 48, 67, 75, 101, 103; Collection of American Literature, Beinecke Library, Yale University, photo by Carl Van Vechten: p. 56; Library of Congress: pp. 10–11, 14, 21, 36, 50, 62, 88, 95, 98, 106; Library of Congress, photo by Arthur Rothstein: pp. 60–61; Library of Congress, photo by Marvin and Morgan Smith: p. 65; Moorland-Spingarn Research Center, Howard University: pp. 13, 31, 92; Schomburg Center for Research in Black Culture, New York Public Library, Astor, Lenox and Tilden Foundations: pp. 34, 39, 82, 97; UPI/Bettmann Archive: pp. 41, 54, 73, 76, 85, 96

JANE FRASER is a Columbia University graduate whose writing has appeared in various publications. A native of Canada, she currently resides in Brooklyn, New York.

NATHAN IRVIN HUGGINS is W.E.B. Du Bois Professor of History and Director of the W.E.B. Du Bois Institute for Afro-American Research at Harvard University. He previously taught at Columbia University. Professor Huggins is the author of numerous books, including *Black Odyssey: The Afro-American Ordeal in Slavery*, *The Harlem Renaissance*, and *Slave and Citizen: The Life of Frederick Douglass*.